FROM ALMEDA TO ZILPHIA:
ARKANSAS WOMEN WHO TRANSFORMED AMERICAN POPULAR SONG

WRITTEN BY **STEPHEN KOCH**

ILLUSTRATED BY **KATHERINE STRAUSE**

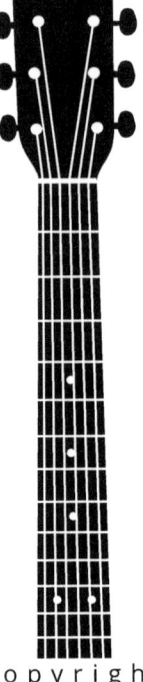

"There's some things they call music [that] to me is really noise. Maybe it's music to someone else. Maybe what's noise to me is music to someone else, and what's music to me is noise.... but I dislike intolerance."

—*Almeda Riddle*

"Music is not trimming! Music is the heart of things— of beliefs, of situations, of struggle, of ideas, of life itself."

—*Zilphia Horton*

Copyright © 2024 by Stephen Koch, arkansongs.org. Art by Katherine Strause, katherinestrause.com. Cover design & interior design and layout by Amy Ashford, ashford-design-studio.com ISBN: 978-1-944528-31-7 Library of Congress Control Number: 217630 / Cataloging in Publication Data applied for. Printed in the United States of America. Please respect authors' rights by not copying without written permission from the publisher, except in the case of reviews. Permission is expressly denied for use of this book's contents for AI training. Contact publisher for permission under any circumstances aside from book reviews. Et Alia Press titles are available at special discounts when purchased in quantity directly from the Press. For details, contact hello@etalia-press.com or the address below. Published in the United States of America by: Et Alia Press PO Box 7948 Little Rock, AR 72217 etaliapress.com

Also by the author:

Louis Jordan: Son of Arkansas, Father of R&B
Join Me In L.A.!: Rock 'N' Roll Adventures (illustrator)
Ozark Murder Ballads Illustrated, Vols. I–III (illustrator)
Music In Arkansas Origins: 200 B.C.–1941 A.D. (writer-narrator)
JUMP! The Louis Jordan Story (playwright)
Encyclopedia of Arkansas Music (contributor)
Arkansas Biography (contributor)

"Music was my refuge."

—*Maya Angelou*

TABLE OF CONTENTS

INTRODUCTION

Dr. Cherisse Jones-Branch **6**

CHAPTERS

"Arkansas," Eva Ware Barnett, Cotton Plant **8**

Maya Angelou, Stamps **13**

Gretha Boston, Crossett **16**

Grace Brim, Biscoe **19**

Maxine Brown, Sparkman / Pine Bluff **22**

Shirley Brown, West Memphis **25**

Carrie Cash, Rison **28**

Carolina Cotton, Craighead County **31**

Iris DeMent, Paragould **35**

Beth Ditto, White County **38**

Bonnie Dodd, Saline County / Hot Springs **41**

Caroline Dye, Newport **45**

Dale Evans, Osceola **48**

Ollie Gilbert, Stone County **51**

Barbara Hendricks, Stephens **54**

Violet Brumley Hensley, Montgomery County **57**

Zilphia Horton, Logan County **60**

Kenni Huskey, Newport **64**

Mable John, Ouachita County **67**

Marjorie Lawrence, Hot Springs **71**

Ketty Lester, Hope **74**

Roberta Martin, Helena **78**

Rose Marie McCoy, Oneida **81**

Patsy Montana, Garland County / Hope **84**

K.T. Oslin, Crossett **87**

Florence Price, Little Rock **91**

Almeda Riddle, Cleburne County / White County **94**

Rosetta Tharpe, Cotton Plant **97**

Vena Townsend, Rose Bud **100**

Sippie Wallace, Jefferson County **103**

AFTERWORD

Erin Enderlin **107**

INTRODUCTION

From Almeda to Zilphia: Arkansas Women Who Transformed American Popular Song is the book we did not know we needed.

Within these pages lies a rich tapestry of stories and experiences from women who contributed to some of the most iconic music in American history. Their expertise spans the length of the 20th and first part of the 21st centuries, as in the case of Eva Ware Barnett who attended a United Daughters of the Confederacy meeting in 1916 before the United States' entry into World War I where members "deplored the fact that Arkansas had no state song."[1] Barnett went home, took pen to paper, and wrote "Arkansas."[2] Adopted as the official state song in 1917, "Arkansas" received international renown when it was endorsed by the Montreal, Quebec, Canada-based Arkansas Club.[3]

Arkansas-connected women influenced American music during some of the most tumultuous times in the nation's history. Arkansas women created popular songs that aided the civil rights movement. Logan County's Zilphia Johnson Horton's labor activism landed her at the Highlander Folk School in Monteagle, Tennessee, where she taught songwriting classes and reworked such songs as "We Shall Overcome" into labor and civil rights anthems.

From Almeda to Zilphia chronicles women who reflect the diversity of the state. Best known as a poet, Maya Angelou, who spent part of her childhood in Stamps, recorded calypso music. Few knew that she traveled singing in *Porgy and Bess* as part of a U.S. State Department-sponsored show. Sparkman country vocalist Maxine Brown wrote "Looking Back to See" in the 1950s and West Memphis native Shirley Brown's Grammy-nominated "Woman to Woman" sold a million copies in the 1970s. Women produced music that spanned the post-World War II years, the 1960s, and beyond and addressed issues beyond romantic relationships.

Arkansas women's musical tastes further varied over time. Crossett's Gretha Boston went from being influenced by music in the African Methodist Episcopal Church to singing with the Manhattan Philharmonic at Carnegie Hall. Barbara Hendricks, born in Stephens, later embarked upon an illustrious career as an international opera singer. Of course, we certainly cannot overlook the women who supported and inspired some of the most famous names in American music. Johnny Cash's mother, Carrie, a Cleveland County native, raised her children in the depths of the Great Depression and New Deal years. She imbued her son with a love of music that profoundly influenced his career.

This collection includes women who moved away from Arkansas to such places as Indiana, Illinois, California, Washington, Oregon, Nashville, Kentucky, and Europe to seek their fortunes as musicians. Arkansas women impacted the music world with their array of diverse experiences, skills, and identities. They represented and touched every part of the state of Arkansas with their musicality, even if they were not musicians themselves. For instance, Jackson County's "Aunt" Caroline Dye was prominently featured in the music of W. C. Handy and the Memphis Jug Band.

There is no shortage of phenomenal and groundbreaking stories among the women chronicled in these pages. One only needs to read the brief but deeply informative vignettes and peruse the list of songs after each to better understand their contributions to Arkansas and American music. In *From Almeda to Zilphia*, Arkansas women heretofore unheralded and uncelebrated in American popular music history are now proudly honored and purposefully featured for their historical musical legacies. We are most fortunate to have this fine book in the world to behold their splendor.

—**Cherisse Jones-Branch, Ph.D.**

1. "Her First Composition Is Made State's Official Song," *Arkansas Gazette,* January 13, 1917, page 4.

2. "New State Song and Its Author," *The Pulaskian*, Little Rock, August 18, 1916, front page.

3. "Is Composer of Arkansas Song," *Arkansas Democrat*, Little Rock, April 27, 1916, page 4; "Around the Statehouse," *The Green Forest Tribune*, Green Forest, Arkansas, January 19, 1917, front page.

Dr. Cherisse Jones-Branch is Dean of the Graduate School and Professor of History at Arkansas State University where she has been employed since 2003. She received her B.A. and M.A. from the College of Charleston, and a Ph.D. from The Ohio State University. A Rural, Women's and African American history scholar, Dr. Jones-Branch is the author of *Crossing the Line: Women and Interracial Activism in South Carolina during and after World War II* and *Better Living By Their Own Bootstraps: Black Women's Activism in Rural Arkansas, 1913–1965*, and is the co-editor of *Arkansas Women: Their Lives and Times* in addition to many articles and essays. She is working on a third book project titled *To Make the Farm Bureau Stronger and Better for All the People: African Americans and the American Farm Bureau Federation: 1920–1966*. She is also the co-editor of the "Rural Black Studies" series for the University of Arkansas Press. Dr. Jones-Branch is a U.S. Army Persian Gulf War Veteran.

"Arkansas"
◆ EVA WARE BARNETT ◆
Cotton Plant

official state song composer, musician, teacher

Many states in the U.S. have easily identifiable, well-known state songs. In Arkansas, it's complicated. But songwriter Eva Ware Barnett of Cotton Plant was there from the start, and after a circuitous journey, her song "Arkansas" is here at the end.

For decades after attaining statehood in 1836, Arkansas existed without an official song. Today, there's an embarrassment of state song riches. And several other would-be official Arkansas songs have been put before the Legislature but failed to pass muster.

Born July 13, 1881, the raven-haired Woodruff County native was a classically-trained pianist who had studied music in New York and abroad before returning to Arkansas to teach at Ouachita Baptist College and Little Rock Conservatory. Soon after, her name would intertwine with state history, even as attempts were made to unravel the two.

Indeed, the story of Arkansas's official state song is a tangled one. An act by the Arkansas Legislature made Barnett's song "Arkansas" official in January 1917. A vocal quartet sang the song to legislators as they made their decision. The approving resolution noted that the song was already "recognized by" most schools "as the State Song." "The air has a lurking melody that will make it a favorite wherever it is heard," *The Pulaskian* newspaper reported in August 1916. Governor Charles Brough—the superlative-prone 25th governor and Mississippi native who later campaigned to nickname Arkansas "The Wonder State"—said it was the most beautiful song he'd ever heard.

However, lost to history is the official impetus to adopt a state song at all. At the time, only a few states had them. It is thought that the completion of the battleship *U.S.S. Arkansas*, commissioned in late 1912, coupled with World War I-era jingoism, were factors in the push to secure a state song for Arkansas. To that point, the commander of the battleship *Arkansas* had even written Barnett a fan letter, telling her how much the ship's crew loved singing her song.

But in granting the song "Arkansas" official status, the Arkansas Legislature apparently failed to secure the song's copyright. Still, years passed without incident until longtime Arkansas Secretary of State Claris Gus "Crip" Hall distributed a free pamphlet statewide featuring the song, as well as prominently featuring Hall's

The "Arkansas Traveler" melody is probably more identified with the state than any other. But in its original form, "Arkansas Traveler" was really as much a comedy routine as a song, with cornball jokes told between musical interludes. So, the official song committee members were tasked to write new lyrics for the old "Arkansas Traveler" tune. No individual has ever claimed responsibility for the lyrics, laying any credit or blame at the feet of "the Arkansas State Song Selection Committee."

Dating from the mid-1800s, "Arkansas Traveler" was an oft-performed stage routine well into the 20th century, while the "Arkansas Traveler" melody remains a classic riff of Americana / folk music. The first known sheet music of the song was published in 1847. A testament to the song's enduring popularity, Arkansas fiddle player Eck Robertson of Delaney recorded a version of "Arkansas Traveler," then already decades old, at his groundbreaking 1922 sessions, which are credited as capturing the first-ever country music recordings. Seventy years later, Michelle Shocked recorded the song with Timbo native Jimmy Driftwood and Bernie Leadon of The Eagles at Mountain View for her acclaimed album of the same name. In the decades between, "Arkansas Traveler" has been recorded and performed by innumerable stage performers and comedians, as well as bluegrass, country, and folk musicians. It's additionally long been heard in movies, cartoons, television, video games, and children's programming.

The wide-ranging term "Arkansas Traveler" could also refer to the tomato of the same name, the honorary title given to notable visitors to the state, the 1938 movie starring Bob Burns, an old brand of fiberglass boats, or the nickname of the state's longstanding minor league baseball team, among several other sundry things.

own name, just before an election year. Armed with the pamphlet, the song's author and legal copyright owner, Barnett, sued the state for damages to her sheet music sales. Although no judgment was issued against the state in this case, both parties girded for further battle. In response, Governor Homer Adkins created a commission in 1943 to get a new state song. A full decade after the initial ownership dispute between the state and Barnett—and 30 years after her song "Arkansas" had been initially named the official song—the song "Arkansas Traveler," credited to Sandy Faulkner, was put forth by the Arkansas Legislature as a replacement.

"Arkansas Traveler," with its boostering, committee-crafted lyrics, served as the official state song from the late 1940s through the early 1960s. However, in another apparent legislative oversight, "Arkansas Traveler" was evidently never officially adopted as the state song. Meanwhile, original state song songwriter Eva Ware Barnett and the state of Arkansas made peace in 1963, and she generously assigned the copyright of her song "Arkansas" to the state.

Thus, a new legislative resolution was put forth, now asserting that the once-beloved song "Arkansas Traveler" was "not conducive to the development of love, respect, and patriotism for our beloved state," while proclaiming Barnett's song "more clearly descriptive of [the state's] attractions, traditions, and loyalties." So, Barnett's "Arkansas" was again made the official state song. That is, if it ever legally wasn't.

However, despite its restored official status as state song, few Arkansas schoolchildren—much less battleship crews—have known or sung Barnett's "Arkansas" since its original dethroning in the 1940s. Barnett died January 20, 1978, in Little Rock at age 96. Meanwhile, some legislators and other citizens wondered aloud if her quaint early 20th century song was too antiquated for modern ears.

In the early 1970s, the song "Arkansas Waltz" asked another musical question: Does the state need an official waltz? A 1971 state Senate resolution sponsored by Virgil Fletcher of Benton unanimously answered yes. Written by Cletus "Slim" Jones and Bill Urfer and sung by Lonsdale native Jones, the song was endorsed by Governor Dale Bumpers and by powerful U.S. Congressman Wilbur D. Mills. But even with a unanimous Senate victory, the officialdom of "Arkansas Waltz" was not considered by the House and thus has been relegated to the dustbin of state history.

Similarly, in the mid-1980s, another song, also called "Arkansas," was put forth in the Arkansas House as a possible new state song replacement for Barnett's "Arkansas," but the motion was subsequently withdrawn.

After the state of Arkansas celebrated its 150th anniversary in 1986, the Arkansas Legislature again ventured into the state song fray. It also did some much-needed official state song legislative housekeeping. The Legislature decreed that henceforth Barnett's song "Arkansas" would be known as the official state anthem. Its rival, the once quasi-official "Arkansas Traveler," was also made an official song, although it would now be known as the state historical song.

Incredibly, two more songs were added to the suddenly crowded pantheon: "Oh, Arkansas," written by Mark Weinstein, Gary Klass, and Terry Rose, and sung by Little Rock musician Rose, and "Arkansas, You Run Deep In Me," written and sung by Wayland Holyfield.

In the intervening years since the two most recent official entries, Holyfield's song in particular has shown staying power. Known for writing songs for the likes of George Strait and Randy Travis, Holyfield was born in Conway County and attended Little Rock's Hall High. He wrote hundreds of songs in his career, but Holyfield said "Arkansas, You Run Deep In Me," written on commission for the old Arkansas Power & Light Company, was his favorite among his vast catalog of songs. For years, "Arkansas, You Run Deep In Me" was the nightly sign-off song for Arkansas public television. The phrase is even painted as a mural near the state Capitol. In 2021, Holyfield gave rights to the song to ACF, the Arkansas Community Foundation, a Little Rock nonprofit.

With so many now to choose from, it's easy to see why many in Arkansas remain fuzzy on their official state song. It's complicated. All of the state's official songs are available for listening at the secretary of state's website, but amid decades of confusion, a 1987 state law clarified that "the Secretary of State shall respond to requests for the state song" with copies of Barnett's song "Arkansas."

This would seem to give the last word, once again, to Eva Ware Barnett—the woman who started it all.

• LISTENING •

"Arkansas" - Eva Ware Barnett
"Arkansas Traveler" - Sandy Faulkner
"Arkansas Traveler" - Eck Robertson
"Arkansas Traveler" - Jimmy Dorsey
"Arkansas Traveler" - Michelle Shocked
"Arkansas Waltz" - Cletus "Slim" Jones
"Oh, Arkansas" - Terry Rose
"Arkansas, You Run Deep In Me" - Wayland Holyfield

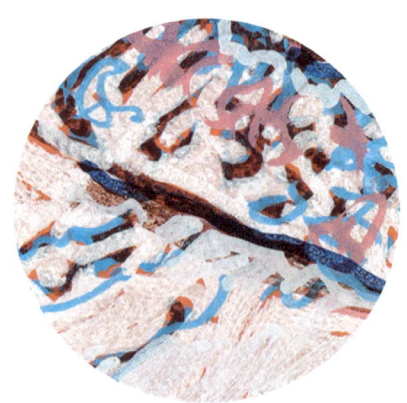

◈ MAYA ANGELOU ◈
Stamps

calypso singer, poet, playwright, author, actor, activist

A trailblazer across the genres, Maya Angelou was born Marguerite Johnson in St. Louis, Missouri, on April 4, 1928. She moved to Stamps when her parents split up. Her father put Marguerite and her brother alone on a train from California to his mother's in Southwest Arkansas's Lafayette County. Her brother was four years old. She was three.

In the American civil rights era, Angelou worked in Dr. Martin Luther King's Southern Christian Leadership Conference. She was also a professor, an Emmy-nominated actress, a Tony-nominated playwright, and a multiple Grammy-winner for her spoken word albums. In 2010, President Barack Obama awarded her the Presidential Medal of Freedom, and in 2022, Angelou appeared on a U.S. quarter, the first Black woman to do so.

Always interested in the arts and in words, Angelou's likely best-known work is *I Know Why The Caged Bird Sings* (Random House, 1969). The book gets its name from a line by poet Paul Laurence Dunbar. And though the autobiographical novel isn't poetry, Angelou, who died May 28, 2014, is largely remembered as a poet, especially due to her reading of a poem at fellow Southwest Arkansawyer Bill Clinton's presidential inauguration and her line of Hallmark greeting cards.

However, less mentioned is her time as a calypso singer, which is even more remarkable with an understanding of the background that led her to the microphone. While living in St. Louis as an adolescent, Angelou was raped. As a result of the trauma, she rarely spoke for several years. When she moved back to Stamps, a teacher there named Beulah Flowers took an interest in her and encouraged her to study literature. Eventually, Angelou spoke again. She would in fact become known for her voice and her use of it to lift others.

In the 1940s, after relocating to San Francisco, California, Angelou studied dance and drama. While still in high school, she reportedly became the city's first Black female streetcar conductor. She'd also become pregnant while in high school, hiding the pregnancy so she could graduate. Mere weeks after the graduation ceremony, she gave birth to her only child, Guy Johnson. Always confident in her dancing ability, dance was her entrée to the stage, and she chose the name Maya Angelou. By the 1950s, Angelou had danced on television variety shows, toured Europe in a production of *Porgy and Bess* sponsored by the U.S. State Department, and performed a calypso-themed stage show. In Paris, she met "music machine" Bob Dorough, a fellow Arkansawyer from Polk County, who helped her hone her act. So, by November 1956, when Angelou made her calypso recordings, she had already lived quite a life, although her best was yet to come.

"I decided to develop my own material," she recalled. "I began making up music for poems I had written years before, and writing new songs that fit the calypso form." Interest in calypso music in the U.S. was at its height from the mid-1950s through the early 1960s. But a decade prior, Brinkley native Louis Jordan, the father of R&B music, helped introduce the sound to stateside audiences and was rewarded with several hits. Like Jordan, Angelou wasn't above employing a faux island-tinged accent to get her musical point across. Angelou gives a nod to Jordan's influence on the genre by recording his 1940s calypso hits "Run Joe" and "Push Ka Pee Shee Pie." "Run Joe," in particular, was a go-to song for her and the opening number in her act: "I played Louis Jordan's record ['Run Joe'] until it was gun-metal gray," she said. She also re-recorded a 1940s-era Louis Jordan / Ella Fitzgerald duet, "Stone Cold Dead In The Market (He Had It Coming)." She additionally makes a couple of appearances in the 1957 musical film revue *Calypso Heat*.

On the *Miss Calypso* album cover, Angelou's statuesque frame is seen dancing barefoot in front of a campfire, wearing a revealing red wrap against the backdrop of an island scene. The album's liner notes falsely state she is 27 years old and Cuban, with her father described as "a full-blooded Watusi." "This is Maya Angelou. This is Miss Calypso. They are one and the same," declare the album's original liner notes.

In *The Heart of a Woman*, a volume of her autobiography, Angelou dismisses her calypso time in light of her other accomplishments as "singing clever little songs only moderately well." Her Tony and Emmy Award nominations, her Pulitzer Prize nomination, her work in the civil rights movement, winning Grammys, and mentoring Oprah Winfrey among legions of others, were still ahead of her. But before all that, Maya Angelou was Miss Calypso. They were one and the same.

• **LISTENING** •

"Peas And Rice" - Maya Angelou
"Stone Cold Dead In the Market (He Had It Coming)" - Maya Angelou
"Push Ka Pee Shee Pie" - Maya Angelou
"Since Me Man Done Gone And Went" - Maya Angelou
"Donkey City" - Maya Angelou
"Run Joe" - Maya Angelou
"Neighbor, Neighbor" - Maya Angelou

GRETHA BOSTON
Crossett

vocalist, actor

Gretha Boston's talents are so varied, she could have excelled as a classical vocalist alone, but additionally became a star of musical theater, and later, television, becoming the first Tony winner in the state.

She was born Gretha Denise Boston on April 18, 1959, in Crossett. The first of seven siblings, she grew up immersed in the music of the A.M.E. church, attending Gates Chapel African Methodist Episcopal Church on Third Avenue in Crossett. Boston also gained notice in the school choir at Crossett High School. She pursued her studies in music and performance at University of North Texas in Denton and the University of Illinois Urbana-Champaign, where she twice won the D'Angelo International Young Artist Competition.

The mezzo-soprano sang with the Manhattan Philharmonic at Carnegie Hall in New York and had many operatic roles — in operas from *Aida* to *Porgy And Bess*, staged at prestigious halls across the country — but largely left her classical and operatic leanings behind to excel in acting and musical theater.

In 1995, Boston won a Tony Award for Best Featured Actress for her role as Queenie in the revival of *Show Boat*, becoming the first Arkansawyer to ever win a Tony.

"In a little town called Crossett, Arkansas, a ballroom is filled with my parents, sister, all five of my brothers, along with a host of other family members and friends. Thank you for always being my safe haven," she said in her acceptance speech.

She was nominated for a Tony Award again in 1999 for *It Ain't Nothin' But The Blues*, and she toured nationally as Bloody Mary in a revival of *South Pacific* in 2002. She was inducted into the Arkansas Black Hall of Fame in 1997. After living in New York City, she settled in Houston, Texas.

In the early 2000s, while still singing in revues, musicals, and concerts, she switched gears again. Boston made a handful of dramatic appearances on television shows such as *Hope & Faith*, *Law & Order*, and *Law & Order: Criminal Intent*. She also sang on PBS and appeared on the *Late Show with David Letterman* and *The Today Show*.

Gretha Boston remains a figure of inspiration for using *all* of one's talents.

• **LISTENING** •

"Blood Done Signed My Name" - Gretha Boston
"I Know I've Been Changed" - Gretha Boston
"Can't Help Lovin' Dat Man" - Gretha Boston
"Coronation Mass" - Gretha Boston
"St. Louis Blues" - Gretha Boston
"I'm Gonna Do What The Spirit Says Do" - Gretha Boston

GRACE BRIM

Biscoe

blues singer, drummer, harmonica player

Loftily billed as "Queen of the Harmonica," Grace Brim made her name as a pioneer of mid-20th century blues music.

Biscoe was a Black-majority town with a population of a few hundred when Grace Millard was born there on July 10, 1923. Biscoe and the larger area became known as a hotbed for blues. Said to be founded by Cherokee settlers in the early 1800s, it by legend was called Fredonia after the Republic of Fredonia independence movement in Mexican Texas. Regardless of its name, Millard took the spirit of her community to heart and became a rarity as a woman harmonica player in a field crowded with men.

Millard was known for her full, rich harmonica tone. Aside from being at home on the harmonica, Millard had other talents, including playing the drums and singing. She recorded with legends of the blues, most often alongside her longtime musical partner and husband, John "Ice Cream Man" Brim of Hopkinsville, Kentucky.

Grace Millard and John Brim married in 1947 and gigged around where they began their relationship in Gary, Indiana, and beyond. She and her husband were a pair, romantically and musically, recording and performing together often. They recorded with pianist Big Maceo Merriweather for Fortune Records of Detroit, Michigan, in 1950, with Grace on vocals. The next year, Grace and John each had a release on Random Records of Chicago, Illinois.

In the early 1950s, Grace and John Brim were billed as John Brim and His Trio with famed blues pianist Sunnyland Slim. Grace also recorded with her husband as John Brim and His Gary Kings, and John Brim and His Stompers, named for John's song, "Gary Stomp." They recorded as The John Brim Trio for J-O-B Records of Chicago, which was the record label that dubbed Grace "Queen of the Harmonica." She also appeared as "Mrs. John Brim." Grace additionally recorded with Snooky Pryor, Eddie Taylor, Jimmy Reed, and fellow Arkansawyer Roosevelt Sykes, among others.

Based in Gary, the Brims had nine children. Grace increasingly left the spotlight to John as she cared for their large family. The couple last appeared together on a single in the 1970s.

After several years of relative domestic quiet, Grace and John Brim got an unexpected boost in the late 1970s when John's song "Ice Cream Man" appeared on rock band Van Halen's self-titled debut. That 1978 album has since sold millions of copies in the U.S. alone. Already a blues standard, "Ice Cream Man" has since become well-known across the genres. While Grace played on her husband's original recorded version of the song, "Ice Cream Man" was deemed too risqué for release at the time, with its suggestive lyrics about satisfying sweet treats.

Grace Millard Brim died June 28, 1999, in Gary, Indiana. She is remembered by students of deep blues music as a groundbreaker of her era.

• LISTENING •

"Man Around My Door" - Grace Brim
"Hospitality Blues" - Grace Brim
"Ice Cream Man" - John Brim
"Ice Cream Man" - Van Halen
"Drinking Woman" - Grace Brim
"Going Down The Line" - Mrs. John Brim

MAXINE BROWN
Sparkman / Pine Bluff

country singer, songwriter

Maxine Brown was a vocalist and songwriter who held her own in the male-dominated world of mid-20th century country music.

Born in Campti, Louisiana, on April 27, 1931, Maxine was the eldest child in the family. Brown made her name singing in the sibling group The Browns, initially with her brother Jim Ed ("J.E."), who was born in Sparkman in Dallas County.

The Brown family moved to Pine Bluff while the children were still small, and later lived in Benton, in their first house with indoor plumbing.

They also lived in Fordyce, Redfield, and Star City.

Growing up in poverty, the family moved often, pursuing work opportunities. The children adored listening to The Grand Ole Opry on the radio, but their radio time was rationed as the family, whose household didn't yet have electricity, had to save the radio's battery. In the process of trying to emulate their country music heroes they heard on the air, the children created their own sibling harmonies.

But Maxine and J.E. were themselves appearing on the radio by the early 1950s, starting with local Pine Bluff station KCLA. And, beginning when Maxine entered J.E. in a talent contest without his knowledge, the pair could be heard on KLRA's "Barnyard Frolic" program live at Robinson Auditorium in Little Rock.

The other integral part of the Brown sound, sister Bonnie, was six years younger than Maxine. At age 17, Bonnie joined Maxine and J.E. in the group, making it a trio and the best-known incarnation of the singing Browns.

"Looking Back To See" was the first-ever song written by Maxine. She didn't think the song was any good, but it landed The Browns a recording contract with Fabor Records. Fabor was a California record label launched in late 1953 by fellow Arkansawyer Fabor Robison. Right out of the gate, it became the trio's first single and first hit in 1954 on Fabor. Although ecstatic about being in show business, The Browns were barely out of their teens and did not sign a contract that was financially favorable to them. Maxine describes The Browns' business relationship with the widely reviled Robison in her autobiography, *Looking Back To See* (University of Arkansas Press, 2005). The chapters "We Get Screwed" and "Screwed Again" detail how Robison allegedly threatened, badgered, and stole royalties from the youths. The sweet harmonies of Maxine, J.E., and Bonnie's

> Fabor Robison was born 1911 in Beebe. Besides The Browns, Robison promoted the early careers of Jim Reeves, Johnny Horton, Floyd Cramer, and future Arkansas state legislator Bobby Lee Trammell. In addition to Fabor Records, Robison owned the Abbott record label. Although many of his performers found success, Robison's alleged poor treatment of artists was widely discussed in country music circles well beyond Maxine Brown's recollections. "When everything went sour, Robison would disappear for a while," wrote author Colin Escott. Robison died in Minden, Louisiana, in 1986.

three voices showcased the group's often tender songs, many of them tales of unrequited love written by Maxine. (Baby sister Norma was the usual fill-in for any member of the trio unable to appear.) Their parents even opened an eatery in Pine Bluff called The Trio Restaurant and Supper Club, and many country music luminaries performed there and enjoyed the cooking of "Momma Brown," a.k.a. Birdie.

The Browns toured with Elvis Presley as his opening act in Presley's pivotal year of 1955. Presley later asked Bonnie to marry him, but she demurred. The next year, the siblings were finally able to leave Robison's Fabor Records, signing to RCA Records in 1956, improving their fortunes as well as allowing the trio to record with the legendary likes of Chet Atkins, Jerry Reed, Roy Huskey Jr., Floyd Cramer, and others.

The year 1959 was a watershed one for The Browns, with their hit "The Three Bells" selling a million copies and being nominated for a Grammy. The Browns joined The Grand Ole Opry in 1963. They stopped performing together in 1967 so Maxine and Bonnie could raise families, but J.E. embarked on a solo career. Maxine also recorded as a solo singer, cutting an album for Chart Records, *Sugar Cane County*, in 1969, and a single called "Is That All There Is" for another label the following year.

Later in the 1970s, Maxine and Bonnie opened up Brown's Recording Studio in Little Rock. In 1977, the two sisters recorded an album with Tom T. Hall called *New Train, Same Rider*.

The original Brown trio of Maxine, Bonnie, and J.E. reunited occasionally over the years. The three returned to The Grand Ole Opry stage in 1990. Later, they recorded a gospel album.

In 2010, Maxine curated *Three Shades of Brown*, a 31-track collection of their songs. Norma, the youngest of the Brown children to sing in the group, had died nearly a decade before. In 2015, The Browns were inducted into The Country Music Hall of Fame, a thrilling validation for the trio. Mere months later, J.E. died. With Bonnie's death the following year, Maxine, the eldest sibling and the acknowledged ringleader of their group, was the last surviving singing Brown. Maxine Brown, the original sister and songwriter who created The Browns, died January 21, 2019.

• LISTENING •

"Looking Back To See" - The Browns
"Here Today And Gone Tomorrow" - The Browns
"The Three Bells" - The Browns
"The Old Lamplighter" - The Browns
"Scarlet Ribbons (For Her Hair)" - The Browns
"It Takes A Long, Long Train With A Red Caboose (To Carry My Blues Away)" - The Browns
"Sugar Cane County" - Maxine Brown
"Is That All There Is" - Maxine Brown

SHIRLEY BROWN
West Memphis

R&B singer with the last big hit at Stax

Nurtured by a blues guitar giant, singing prodigy Shirley Brown gave legendary Memphis record label Stax its final million-seller.

Born January 6, 1947, in West Memphis, Brown moved to Illinois at the age of nine. While still young, she'd sung with such notable blues performers as Little Milton and Albert King. King, like Brown, also lived in Crittenden County, and the guitarist is buried there. Hearing her sing at an Illinois club when she was just 14, King took young Brown under his wing. Brown then toured with the Albert King revue for several years. Brown described him as a fatherly figure. King was reportedly strict that she have a tutor and do her homework. He recorded for Stax Records of Memphis, Tennessee, and it was King who brought Brown to Stax. And it was Stax, in turn, that brought fame to Brown.

In the mid-1970s, the storied Stax label was primarily owned by Brinkley native Al Bell and was in financial trouble. "What they owed me on paper," Bell recalled in a 2000 interview with *Arkansongs*, "they sent back to me in records. So there was no money forthcoming. What [record distributors] had been doing was taking the product in, warehousing it, bleeding the marketplace— and bleeding *me*—and doing what they do when they get ready to take over a corporation. They didn't call it a hostile takeover back then, but that's what it was about."

Enter Shirley Brown.

In an attempt to save the label that he'd launched in the late 1950s and left in the early 1970s, former Stax owner Jim Stewart returned to the Stax label to co-produce Brown in March 1974 along with famed drummer Al Jackson Jr. The first song Brown recorded at Stax, "Woman To Woman," tells the story of a wife who confronts another woman in a phone conversation after finding a phone number in her husband's pants pocket. Written by James Banks, Eddie Marion, and Henderson Thigpen, "Woman To Woman" had already been rejected by another Stax artist, Inez Foxx, but became Stax's last major hit song. While Foxx allegedly didn't like the spoken word introduction to the song, Brown made the intro her own.

"Woman to woman, if you've ever been in love," she then sings in the chorus, "Then you'll know just how I feel."

After years of toiling as a fairly unknown touring singer, "Woman To Woman" made Brown a solo star. Appearing on Stax's Truth subsidiary label, "Woman To Woman" was nominated for a Grammy for Best Female R&B Performance, sold over a million copies, and spawned at least two answer songs: Lonnie Youngblood's "Man To Woman" and Barbara Mason's "From His Woman To You," which used new lyrics over the original melody and reached #3 on the R&B charts in December 1974.

Country singer Barbara Mandrell had her first crossover hit with "Woman To Woman" in 1978. R&B singer Jewell's 1994 version sampled Brown's original.

By 1974, the one-time R&B success story Stax had only four top ten hits. By the end of the year, Stax Records purchased the small pressing plant of a small record label, Rimrock, in the Cleburne County town of Concord. Rimrock Records was owned by Wolf Bayou native Wayne Raney, himself a former country music star. But Rimrock's tiny output could not fit the needs of a large label like Stax. And when Brown's second hit song, "It Ain't No Fun," gained steam in spring 1975, the Rimrock pressing plant was working around the clock to meet production schedules.

Brown's attendant album, also titled *Woman To Woman*, was her first full-length album and featured another West Memphis native, Wayne Jackson of the Memphis Horns, on trumpet. Brown's output from this late period of Stax showed the label was still capable of producing hits and engaging material despite its financial problems.

But it wasn't enough to save Stax.

The label's bankruptcy, tragic for many artists, disrupted the career of new Stax star Brown, too. Bell attempted to move the company to Little Rock, but no one could see the vision. Brown never again reached such heights as in the mid-1970s, but she remained a concert draw and recording artist, releasing eight albums from the late 1980s through the early 2000s on the Malaco label of Jackson, Mississippi.

Unlike the original Stax, the noted Memphis record label she gave a final million-selling boost to, Shirley Brown's career continued into the 21st century.

• **LISTENING** •

"Woman To Woman" - Shirley Brown
"It Ain't No Fun" - Shirley Brown
"So Glad To Have You" - Shirley Brown
"Love Starved" - Shirley Brown
"When, Where, And What Time" - Shirley Brown
"Dirty Feelin'" - Shirley Brown
"From His Woman To You" - Barbara Mason
"Woman To Woman" - Barbara Mandrell
"Woman To Woman" - Jewell

CARRIE CASH
Rison

literally and figuratively made Johnny Cash

Johnny Cash has fans across the genres and the generations. Born in South Arkansas and raised in Northeast Arkansas, few artists command broader recognition. An influence worldwide, Cash's own earliest musical influence was close to home—his mother, Carrie.

Born Carrie Cloverlee Rivers March 13, 1904, in Rison, she was raised in the Pentecostal Church of God. With her church's services heavily focused on music, she developed a love of gospel melodies and hymns and regarded music as one of god's gifts.

"Johnny" was born J.R., initials which didn't stand for anything, in 1932 in Cleveland County, the same place where she and J.R.'s father Ray were from, as well as J.R.'s grandparents. With particular encouragement from his mom, J.R. and the whole family grew up singing.

Beyond her own personal musical contributions to her son, Carrie also pushed the impoverished family to buy an extravagance—a radio from Sears, Roebuck and Co. It offered the diversion of music and dreams of a world beyond field work. J.R. would have been only four, but he said he remembered the first song he ever heard on the radio, "Hobo Bill's Last Ride" by Jimmie Rogers. Radio was how they first learned of President Franklin Roosevelt's government land program and community launching in Northeast Arkansas called the Dyess Colony. The Cashes were approved for the whites-only New Deal program and moved from the Kingsland area to Mississippi County to join it. Families were each given a house, barn, cow, mule, chicken coop, and 20 or 40 acres to clear and plant.

For the arduous winter drive north on rough roads, Carrie and the children slept in the back of the truck that was hauling the family's possessions. Johnny later said "I Am Bound For The Promised Land" was the first song he ever sang, and it was sung as the family migrated to Dyess. "Sometimes mama would cry, and sometimes she'd sing," he recalled of the journey in his autobiography. "And sometimes it was hard to tell which was which."

Carrie called her son's affinity for singing and music "the gift." As with the radio, she pushed for another extravagance—a piano, which the family sang around. In a famous family story, Carrie tried to get him voice lessons, but the teacher didn't want to spoil the child's natural tal-

ents with training. Carrie also showed her son guitar basics.

The family radio continued as a mainstay, too. When Johnny was a teen working the fields, he was given an extra 15-minute midday break so he could listen to the *Louvin Brothers' High Noon Roundup* on WMPS in Memphis, Tennessee. At night, he'd listen to stations in New Orleans, Louisiana; Cincinnati, Ohio; Chicago, Illinois; and Wheeling, West Virginia. He'd make his own radio debut on KLCN in Blytheville in his home state.

Cash listened to the expected country forefathers like the Louvins, Roy Acuff, Ernest Tubb, Eddy Arnold, and Hank Williams, but also to pop crooner Bing Crosby and bluesman Pink Anderson. One of his lifelong favorites was gospel guitarist and fellow Arkansawyer Rosetta Tharpe (see page 97).

After Johnny's voice changed, Carrie said it sounded exactly like her father's. Carrie's dad and Johnny's maternal grandfather, John Lewis Rivers, born in 1866, taught the shape-note system and four-part harmony singing in church.

As Johnny began performing as a musician, his early sets included such gospel songs as "Peace In The Valley."

Cash and the Tennessee Two first auditioned at Sun Records with their version of Jimmie Davis and the Sunshine Boys' then-current gospel hit, "I Was There When It Happened." But label owner Sam Phillips didn't like it and told him to come back with something more original. That he did.

Carrie furthered and supported her son's career in other ways beyond her enormous musical influence on him. She even made his initial flashy stage outfits. In fact, Carrie didn't like her son, later nicknamed "The Man In Black," to wear the black stage clothing that became his trademark. She thought a pop of color would do him good. For the last decade of her life, Carrie ran the gift shop at the House of Cash in Tennessee. As was typical of her support of her son's career, the gift shop was her idea.

Carrie Rivers Cash, better known as Johnny Cash's mom, died March 11, 1991, just shy of her 87th birthday. The piano still sits in the Cash family home in Dyess, both lovingly restored by Arkansas State University. As a lifelong lover of music, Carrie must have been pleased to see the pinnacle of fame her son achieved with "the gift." Especially since she was the first one to see and nurture it.

• LISTENING •

"I Am Bound For The Promised Land" - Johnny Cash
"Man In Black" - Johnny Cash
"I Was There When It Happened" - Jimmie Davis with the Sunshine Boys
"Alabama" - The Louvin Brothers
"I Am Bound For The Promised Land" - Hank Williams
"Hobo Bill's Last Ride" - Jimmie Rodgers

CAROLINA COTTON
Craighead County

country musician, singer, yodeler, songwriter

Yodeling star of film, television, and stage, and a pioneering Western swing musician too, Carolina Cotton was born Helen Hagstrom on October 20, 1925, in Cash. She grew up in Northeast Arkansas in Craighead County on a multi-generational family farm with her parents, Fred and Helen. The Hagstroms had immigrated to the U.S. from Sweden and grew cotton, peanuts, and other crops. During the Depression, her father moved the family from their Arkansas farm to San Francisco, California.

As a little girl in California, she studied dance and sang. From a young age, Hagstrom appeared on Bay Area radio programs and sang. Unlike many yodelers, she did not yodel as a young child. Her impressive technique only emerged in her late teens as cowboy movies became popular. With both the look and the talent, she pursued a twin track to fame, both in film and as a singer, and made her mark in both.

Her biggest hit was the jokey pseudo-autobiographical song "Three Miles South of Cash (in Arkansas)," which has fun with some Arkansas stereotypes. The lyrics in part go: "Ain't got no electricity, but that's just where I want to be, three miles south of Cash in Arkansas /

Bandleader Donnell Clyde "Spade" Cooley was born in Grand, Oklahoma, and was a pioneer in the genre of Western swing music. He got his start playing fiddle in the big band of Jimmy Wakely, the crooning cowboy and movie star from Mineola. Cooley took over the Jimmy Wakely band when Wakely got a film contract. Cooley became a recording star in his own right and appeared in dozens of films, including as the stand-in for Roy Rogers. Cooley's groundbreaking early television program launched in 1948 and was eventually broadcast coast to coast and won an Emmy. Meanwhile, his influential band launched the career of Tex Williams as well as that of Carolina Cotton.

Cooley's career ended in shambles in 1961 after he brutally murdered his second wife in front of his 14-year-old daughter. It was just a year after Cooley had received a star on the Hollywood Walk of Fame. California Governor Ronald Reagan fought for his parole, but Cooley died in prison in late 1969.

The *I'm From Arkansas* film also features Jimmy Wakely, who, like Carolina Cotton, actually was from Arkansas. Wakely was born in 1914 in the unincorporated community of Mineola in Howard County.

Wakely's band gave Carolina Cotton her musical start, although Wakely left the band to pursue film stardom as a singing cowboy. But Wakely's velvet-voiced crooning set him on a path beyond cowboy songs and movies. His duets with pop singer Margaret Whiting made for some of the first genre crossover hits. The Country Music Foundation credits Wakely with introducing cheating songs into the country music canon in the late 1940s with his titles "Slippin' Around" and "One Has My Name, The Other Has My Heart."

Wakely recorded several Christian faith-based songs, as well as seasonal recordings. His 1950 hit "Peter Cottontail" remains an Easter favorite; Wakely's yuletide songs became a staple of his multi-faceted career. He recorded both religious and secular Christmas songs, many released on his own label, Shasta Records. In fact, despite his decades of recordings, appearances on radio, television, film, and even in comic books bearing his name, holiday music is how many country and pop fans remember the name Jimmy Wakely. He died in 1982.

General store and a cotton gin, little ole jail my pappy's in, three miles south of Cash in Arkansas."

Three miles south of Cash, the song explains, is a place with "gnats and skeeters buzzing around" where there "ain't no use for a telephone, [since] no one ever stays at home" and "all the gals have too much hospitality." The narrator ultimately decides "I don't care what happens there, I ain't going back because I ain't got the railroad fare."

However sleepy life may have been in her old Arkansas hometown, things came fast to Hagstrom and her burgeoning career as an artist through the 1940s and 1950s. She appeared in a dizzying number of B-movie Westerns, early music videos, and early television programs. She also made personal appearances, and performed live on the radio, on recordings for several different labels, and in concerts.

A nod to her skills and looks, Hagstrom was nicknamed "The Yodeling Blonde Bombshell." She also eventually got a new stage name. At first, she was billed only as "Carolina" when she sang. Later, a radio contest was held to pick her new last name of "Cotton."

Hagstrom / Cotton could play several instruments, including lap steel, filling in when her male bandmates were drafted into World War II. In the mid-1940s, she got a break and began singing with the Spade Cooley Orchestra, one of the pioneering bands of Western swing music. She can be seen playing upright bass in a promo film for the Cooley band's version of the chestnut "Take Me Back To Tulsa."

Cotton's film career is said to have begun with a chance encounter with Oklahoma songwriter and ukulele player Johnny Marvin. Marvin was so taken with her that he offered her a part in a movie he was involved in called *Sing, Neighbor, Sing*. From there, Cotton appeared in 1944's *I'm From Arkansas*, set in fictional Pitchfork, Arkansas. She shows off her yodeling skills in two songs in the film, "Yodel Mountain" and "I Love To Yodel."

Cotton signed with Columbia the next year, appearing in *Outlaws of the Rockies*, released that fall. Western movies quickly became her specialty. In fact, Cotton eventually appeared in so many films within the genre that she acquired another nickname—"Queen of the Range." The massive mid-20th century trend of all things cowboy surely helped.

Less than a year after joining Spade Cooley's band, Cotton married the band's bass player, Deuce Spriggens. The two formed their own band and took a few other sidemen from the Cooley band with them. Typical of her breakneck pace, Cotton and Spriggens recorded, had their own radio program, and even starred in a 1946 film called *Cowboy Blues* before divorcing.

Cotton signed with Cincinnati, Ohio's King Records in 1946, and was sometimes paired with the band of Hank Penny, the label's top country act. In 1950, she signed with M-G-M Records, another label with a large presence in country music. There, she performed and recorded with the *other* giant of Western swing music besides Cooley—Bob Wills. Cotton and Wills and his Texas Playboys even re-cut her signature song, "3 Miles South Of Cash (In Arkansas)." "Three Miles South Of Cash" was also recorded by Floyd and Lloyd, the singing Armstrong Twins, of DeWitt.

Cotton's last films were in 1952: *Blue Canadian Rockies* and *Apache Country*, both with Gene Autry. She also took over a children's amusement park in Compton, California, calling it Carolina Cotton's Tiny Town. She made personal appearances there, along with other cowboy stars.

In 1956, she married again and had two children with musician Bill Ates. They later divorced. She also became a teacher, last teaching in Bakersfield, California. But she didn't leave her former life as an entertainer behind. She maintained a solid schedule of public appearances, appearing at cowboy film festivals and the like through her later years. In fact, Hagstrom never stopped promoting the Carolina Cotton name—even if she did get it in a contest.

Helen Hagstrom died June 10, 1997, but the accomplishments of "The Yodeling Blonde Bombshell" and "Queen of The Range," Carolina Cotton, ring on.

• LISTENING •

"Nola" - Carolina Cotton
"Yodel Mountain" - Carolina Cotton, from the 1944 film *I'm From Arkansas*
"I Love To Yodel" - Carolina Cotton, from the 1944 film *I'm From Arkansas*
"Three Miles South Of Cash (In Arkansas)" - Carolina Cotton with The Bob Wills Orchestra
"Three Miles South of Cash (In Arkansas)" - The Armstrong Twins
"Take Me Back To Tulsa" - Carolina Cotton with The Spade Cooley Orchestra
"Mockingbird Yodel" - Carolina Cotton with The Hank Penny Band
"I Been Down In Texas" - Deuce Spriggens and Carolina Cotton

IRIS DeMENT
Paragould

singer, songwriter

Iris DeMent of Paragould became a gospel / folk sensation in the 1990s. Born January 5, 1961, she grew up in a farming, musical, and religious family, and was the youngest of 14 children. Gospel music was the order of the day in her Pentecostal household. Her father played the fiddle, and her brothers, sisters, and mother played piano and sang. Despite her Arkansas origins, DeMent said she actually didn't hear much secular folk or country music until after the family moved to Cypress, California.

DeMent dropped out of high school but later took some college courses. She worked menial jobs and played acoustic guitar at coffeehouses as she honed her songwriting. In the late 1980s, she relocated to Nashville, Tennessee, to become a performer. Folk and country music legends Jerry Douglas, Emmylou Harris, and Roy Huskey Jr. all appeared on DeMent's debut album, *Infamous Angel*, which was originally released on folk label Rounder Records of Cambridge, Massachusetts.

With songs like "Mama's Opry," DeMent's debut is largely a celebration of her Northeast Arkansas roots and family. DeMent's mother, Flora Mae DeMent, even gets a lead vocal turn on *Infamous Angel*'s closer, "Higher Ground." Meanwhile, the opener, "Let The Mystery Be," has been covered by several artists, including 1990s alternative rock band 10,000 Maniacs and blues guitarist Alice Stuart. DeMent's version was used in the 1993 film *Little Buddha* and as the theme for television's *The Leftovers* in 2015.

She followed up *Infamous Angel* less than a year later in spring 1994 with *My Life*. By then, she was an acclaimed singer-songwriter with a hot record on a major label, having signed to Warner Brothers, which re-released *Infamous Angel*. The album *My Life* seemed to harken back to her early days in Arkansas. It also continued DeMent's rise, being nominated for a Grammy for Best Contemporary Folk Album. Two years passed before DeMent's next record, *The Way I Should*, which found her lyrical and musical palette expanding beyond her folky roots.

In 1995, the song "Our Town" from *Infamous Angel* closed out the series finale of the Emmy-winning television show *Northern Exposure*.

Also through the 1990s, DeMent sang harmony and duets with notable artists such as Emmylou Harris, Tom Paxton, Nanci Griffith, Randy Scruggs, and Steve

Earle, but the smooth-crooning Greene County native's most frequent, and perhaps incongruous, duet partner was craggy-voiced John Prine. She sings on four tracks on Prine's 1999 album, *In Spite of Ourselves*, and on two from Prine's 2016 album, *For Better, For Worse*.

In 1999, *Infamous Angel* was named one of *Rolling Stone* magazine's Essential Recordings of the 1990s, solidifying her ubiquity in the decade. Eight years passed, however, between her third and fourth albums. The fourth, *Lifeline*, had but one original composition.

After her explosive early breakout years, the 21st century was quieter for DeMent. She could be heard singing in the closing credits of the 2010 movie remake of fellow Arkansawyer Charles Portis's novel, *True Grit*, and she appeared in the 2000 movie *Songcatcher*. Fans had to wait eight years for DeMent's next album of original songs with the release of *Sing The Delta* in 2012. 2015 saw the release of DeMent's sixth album, *The Trackless Woods*, inspired by the poems of 20th century Ukranian poet Anna Akhmatova. *Workin' On A World*, released in 2023, continued her trajectory of slyly yet maturely tackling issues that resonate with her, like gun violence and human rights, and helped solidify DeMent's transition from 1990s "It Girl" into a respected folk music legend.

With her vocals always crafted "to lend attention to the song, rather than herself," Little Rock novelist Kevin Brockmeier said Iris DeMent "can seem as if she has lived an entire life inside every note she delivers."

• **LISTENING** •

"Let The Mystery Be" - Iris DeMent
"Our Town" - Iris DeMent
"Higher Ground" - Iris DeMent
"Mama's Opry" - Iris DeMent
"Fifty Miles of Elbow Room" - Iris DeMent
"Leaning On The Everlasting Arms" - Iris DeMent
"Easy's Gettin' Harder Every Day" - Iris DeMent

BETH DITTO
White County

singer, writer, actor, fashion designer

Beyond being a musician, vocalist Beth Ditto emerged as a fashion designer, an actress, and an important voice in the queer community, all launched from her time as lead vocalist in the band Gossip.

Born Mary Beth Patterson on February 19, 1981, in White County, she lived in Judsonia and Georgetown. After her mother Velmyra married Homer Ditto, Beth took the last name of her stepfather who helped raise her. But Beth was often on her own. She's described an impoverished home life with abuse and little adult stability.

She started singing at age six, loving music and even thinking she would be a singer when she grew up. Her first rock band was called Little Miss Muffett. "It was so exciting, this whole music thing," she recalled in her autobiography. "And up until then everything in Arkansas had been so boring."

Multi-instrumentalist Nathan "Brace Paine" Howdeshell, also a White County native, played guitar and keyboards. "It was Nathan who brought the whole scene together," she said. His early bands included Mrs. Garrett and Space Kadet. In high school, Ditto recalls Howdeshell wearing 3-piece polyester suits and Buddy Holly glasses, but Ditto herself would also become known for her cutting-edge look, including bright colors, outsized silhouettes, dramatic hairstyles, and bold makeup. Drummer Kathy Mendonca, also of Searcy, "just hung around with all her hair in her face, projecting cool, radical wisdom." Together, Mendonca, Ditto, and Howdeshell formed the dance / rock trio Gossip.

The band first got together in Olympia, Washington, after Ditto joined her Arkansas friends in the Pacific Northwest: "I didn't belong in Arkansas; none of us did." Serendipitously, a member of famed Olympia-based rock band Sleater-Kinney saw the new band at a gig and was impressed. Incredibly, Gossip had played just a few shows when the trio was invited on a national tour with the high-profile Sleater-Kinney, now considered one of the key U.S. rock groups of the era and pioneers of the "riot grrrl" genre. The first show on the Sleater-Kinney tour was at the famed Seventh Street Entry in Minneapolis, Minnesota. The maximum capacity of the venue was nearly the population of Ditto's old hometown.

Following a 1999 EP on K Records, Gossip's first full-length, *That's Not What I Heard*, was released on Kill

Rock Stars, which was also Sleater-Kinney's record label. Ditto was only 19. After another EP, *Arkansas Heat*, Gossip released *Movement*, which Ditto called the band's "first grown-up record," and toured Scotland.

In what Ditto said was "the saddest moment the band had ever had," original Gossip drummer Kathy Mendonca left the trio in 2005. The band's 2006 breakthrough album, *Standing In The Way of Control*, with new drummer Hannah Blilie, saw Gossip gaining attention internationally. The trio then issued a live album, *Undead In NYC*. *Music For Men*, Gossip's 2009 follow-up, was produced by Rick Rubin and recorded at his legendary Shangri-La Studios in Malibu, California, for Columbia Records. In the late 1970s, the studio was co-owned by Arkansawyer Levon Helm and The Band. In May 2012, Gossip released its fifth full-length album, called *A Joyful Noise*. It reached number three in France, number two in Germany, and number one in Switzerland.

While Gossip maintained a high profile overseas, both Ditto and Howdeshell continued to work with Arkansas musicians, especially their fellow White County natives, including Bonnie Montgomery and Isaac Alexander of Searcy, and Greg Spradlin of Pangburn.

In early 2016, Ditto confirmed the dissolution of Gossip. But Ditto had already made a notable name on her own. She became known as a staunch advocate for the queer community. Her advice column on body image "What Would Beth Ditto Do?" appeared in *The Guardian*. She launched plus-size fashion lines for Evans and Forever 21, modeled in Paris, and collaborated with Jean-Paul Gaultier and MAC. In 2012, her memoir *Coal To Diamonds* was published by Spiegel & Grau. In 2013, she married her longtime girlfriend, Kristin Ogata, divorcing five years later. Gossip reformed for one-off shows, while Ditto went solo, releasing *Fake Sugar* in 2017. She also pursued an acting career, portraying a country singer on the television show *Monarch*.

In March 2024, Gossip released *Real Power*, its first new album in a dozen years, proving Beth Ditto rocks on.

• **LISTENING** •

"Arkansas Heat" - Gossip
"Swing Low" - Gossip
"Got All This Waiting" - Gossip
"Lily White Hands" - Gossip
"In And Out" - Beth Ditto
"Oo La La" - Beth Ditto
"Love In Real Life" - Beth Ditto

BONNIE DODD
Saline County / Hot Springs

songwriter, steel guitar player

Bonnie Dodd of Saline County and Hot Springs became known as a songwriter and steel guitar player, particularly in country and Western swing music. Nicknamed "Little Blossom" by iconic singing cowboy Tex Ritter, her songs of heartbreak have been recorded by everyone from country music legend Hank Williams to the family gospel group The Staple Singers ("I'll Take You There").

She was born Bonnie Modena Dodd on January 9, 1914, in Saline County, the dark-haired youngest of four siblings and the daughter of cotton farmers. The Dodd family farmed in Central Arkansas and East Texas before leaving agriculture in the early 1920s for the city life of Hot Springs. There, Bonnie's mother worked on the city's famed Bathhouse Row at the Ozark Bathhouse, while her father became a barber.

During high school, Dodd worked in a Hot Springs grocery store and also worked on her music. A musical partnership with Murray Lucas saw the pair performing on the legendary Hot Springs radio station KTHS.

Dodd graduated from Hot Springs High School in 1932. She and Murry Lucas continued performing to-

With its call letters standing for "Kum To Hot Springs," radio station KTHS initially broadcast out of the Arlington Hotel in downtown Hot Springs, launching in 1924. KTHS featured many live performers of note beyond Bonnie Dodd, including Patsy Montana (see page 84), and the radio debut of the comedy team Lum and Abner. It eventually became the state's first 50,000 watt station, the maximum allowed in the U.S.

After nearly four decades, KTHS morphed into the Little Rock radio powerhouse KAAY. With its strong and wide signal, KAAY's own deep history began just weeks after the 1962 switchover of the stations, broadcasting U.S. propaganda into the Caribbean during the Cuban Missile Crisis. "The Mighty 1090" was also original home of *Beaker Street*. An overnight program, *Beaker Street* was one the first underground rock shows, helping break bands like Black Oak Arkansas nationally.

Its signal has been documented in some 40 states and nearly 30 countries, with it being one of the longest continually-licensed stations in Arkansas, and one of the most influential stations in the country.

gether for several more years, including on other notable Midwestern U.S. radio stations such as KMOX in St. Louis, Missouri, and on the *National Barn Dance* on WLS in Chicago, Illinois.

In the 1940s, Dodd came into her own as a songwriter and collaborator. She joined the band of Jimmie Davis as its steel guitar player. Davis was the governor of Louisiana but better known for his song, "You Are My Sunshine." Dodd wrote songs with Davis and Charles Mitchell, and she soon began enjoying her own country chart hits—an all too rare feat for a female songwriter in country music.

Also in the 1940s, Dodd began her best-known musical partnership with singer / actor Tex Ritter. Ritter was one of the most popular singing cowboys of the era, appearing in some 70 films. He later was a founding member of the Country Music Association and a lifetime member of The Grand Ole Opry. He was also the father of John Ritter of *Three's Company* and *Sling Blade* fame. It was Tex Ritter who gave Dodd the nickname "Little Blossom," a nod to her looks and small stature. In 1945, Dodd's song "You Will Have To Pay" became a number one hit for Ritter.

Many of Dodd's songs speak of heartbreak, with titles like "If It's Wrong To Love You," "I Dreamed Of An Old Love Affair," and "I'll Just Kiss Your Picture Tonight." Dodd's song, "Don't Say Goodbye If You Love Me," goes "They tell me today you are going far away, just to make you a name / They tell me that you're discontented, and that you are searching for fame."

In particular, Dodd's song "Be Careful of Stones That You Throw" has resonated over the decades with artists across the genres. The song tugs at the heartstrings with a tragic tale of a car wreck, even as it's a moralizing diatribe against harsh gossipy talk: A woman who'd been criticized by her neighbor is killed while saving that neighbor's child from being hit by a passing car. Its chorus goes "A tongue can accuse and carry bad news / The seeds of distrust it will sow / But unless you've made no mistakes in your life / Be careful of stones that you throw."

"Be Careful of Stones That You Throw" was first recorded by Little Jimmy Dickens in 1949, who was riding high that year with his now-classic "Take An Old Cold Tater (And Wait)."

Due to poor health, Dodd retreated from the music

The somber "Be Careful of Stones That You Throw" was a marked contrast from Little Jimmy Dickens's trademark lighter material like "Take An Old Cold Tater (And Wait)" and "May The Bird of Paradise Fly Up Your Nose." "Be Careful of Stones That You Throw" has since been covered by country artists ranging from Red Sovine and Porter Wagoner to Waylon Jennings, Hank Williams Jr., and David Allan Coe. American doo-wop singer Dion even had a hit with the song in the early 1960s, and in 1965, so did The Staple Singers. The Staple Singers' version of the song is included on the soundtrack of the 1996 film *Bastard Out of Carolina*, adapted from Dorothy Allison's defining 1992 Southern novel. Bob Dylan and The Band recorded it during their "Basement Tapes" sessions in 1967. Probably the most famous version of the song was cut in 1952 by Hank Williams as Luke The Drifter, Williams's moralizing alter ego who specialized in recitation songs. Dylan, a big fan of Williams as Luke The Drifter, likely learned of the song through Williams.

business in later years. She never married, living in a house with her sister Elva in Southern California for nearly 40 years. In her final years, Dodd was homebound.

Bonnie Modena "Little Blossom" Dodd died November 2, 1984, in San Diego, California, at age 70. Dodd is buried in Antioch Cemetery in her native Saline County. Her tombstone reads: "Earth has no sorrows that heaven cannot heal."

The extent of her pioneering contributions to country music and Western swing as both a performer and a songwriter remain under-recognized. However, Dodd's 1930s-era steel-bodied National Resonator guitar is on display at the Country Music Hall of Fame in Nashville, Tennessee, and she was mentioned on the inaugural Arkansas Music Trail plaque recognizing KTHS radio, which was dedicated in May 2024 at the Arlington Hotel in Hot Springs.

• LISTENING •
"Be Careful of Stones That You Throw" - Hank Williams (as Luke The Drifter)
"I'll Just Kiss Your Picture Tonight" - Tex Ritter
"Don't Say Goodbye If You Love Me" - Jimmie Davis
"Be Careful of Stones That You Throw" - David Allan Coe
"If It's Wrong To Love You" - Charles Mitchell & His Orchestra
"Be Careful of Stones That You Throw" - Bob Dylan and The Band
"You Will Have To Pay" - Tex Ritter
"I Dreamed of An Old Love Affair" - Jimmie Davis
"Be Careful of Stones That You Throw" - The Staple Singers

CAROLINE DYE
Newport

seer, businesswoman, muse of the blues

Caroline Dye was not a musician, but one of the most prominent women of her era, and she figures into several key pieces of American popular song.

No one is sure when she was born; some say as early as 1810, while some estimates of her death are as late as 1944. Most agree she died in 1918. But one thing not in question in her often mysterious and shadowy life is her reputation as a psychic seer.

She was born Caroline Tracy to enslaved parents; some say in Jackson County's Bird Township, while others claim she was a South Carolina native. Little is known about her parents. In 1867, after the U.S. Civil War when she was freed, Caroline married Martin Dye of Sulphur Rock in Independence County. The family lived in Jackson County's Elgin. Their daughter, Mary, died in infancy, but over the years, they raised several other children in their home.

Dye apparently had "the gift" even when she was young, but as an adult became nationally known for her abilities. She didn't use a crystal ball, seldom read palms, and wouldn't help those who sought romantic advice. However, she often utilized a deck of cards, and as W.C. Handy's lyric about her goes, the "cards don't lie." Dye's specialty was the recovery of lost or stolen items; her ability to locate missing livestock was said to be especially uncanny. Dye never advertised, or even charged for her services, but accepted gratuities. A landowner, investor, and a rich and notable woman, perhaps not even Dye herself could have foreseen how successful she would become.

Around the turn of the century, they moved to Newport, living on Remmel Avenue. Dye received so many visitors into her home that she began serving food. The train into town from Memphis, Tennessee, was nicknamed by locals as the "Caroline Dye Special." She would get letters from all over the region bearing requests and, most usually, money. Folklorist John Quincy Wolf Jr. wrote that, in her heyday, Dye was so well-known in the South, "it was doubtful even the name of President [Woodrow] Wilson was more generally known."

Composer W.C. Handy, who called himself "The father of the blues," said Dye was "the gypsy" mentioned in his 1914 song, "St. Louis Blues," performed by Cab Calloway, Louis Armstrong, Bessie Smith, and dozens of others. "St. Louis Blues" was among the first blues songs to have popular commercial success, and it became a standard in jazz and blues. Nine years later, with Dye's mystic reputation further solidified, Handy wrote about Dye again, this time mentioning her by name in his 1923 song, "Sundown Blues."

In May 1930, the influential Memphis Jug Band recorded its own ode to Dye, but the song came out titled "Aunt Caroline Dyer Blues." It also places her hometown in Newport News, a city in Virginia—and the song's music, and a verse, are lifted from the band's 1927 song "Newport News Blues."

Thirty years after the Memphis Jug Band recorded the "Aunt Caroline Dyer Blues," bandleader Will Shade had this to say about her: "White and colored would go to her. You sick in bed, she raise the sick. Had that much brains. Smart lady. That's the kind of woman she was. Aunt Caroline Dye, she was the worst woman in the world. Had that much sense."

Handy said he got some of his lyrics from folk sayings, and 'Going to see Aunt Caroline' was a catchphrase, which may help explain why the name Caroline Dye appears in still other blues songs, including Johnnie Temple's "Hoodoo Woman," recorded in 1937. Temple gets both Dye's name and hometown correct, singing, "I'm going to Newport, just to see Aunt Caroline Dye." Dye is also notably referenced in the better-known blues song, "Wang Dang Doodle," popularized by Crittenden County resident Howlin' Wolf and also recorded by Koko Taylor, among many others. The line goes, "Tell Peg and Caroline Dye, we gonna have a time." The same verse also mentions Walnut Ridge-born bluesman Washboard Sam.

One of the most celebrated women ever to live in the Midsouth, Dye's tombstone calls her "The Sunbeam of the World," and lists her death as September 26, 1918, at 108 years old. She's buried in Gum Cemetery in Newport. However, some scholars don't even agree on this, with a competing burial place said to be at Gum Grove Cemetery near Walnut Grove in Van Buren County. With only one known photo of her, people claiming to be Dye lived on for decades, performing readings, accepting gratuities, and adding to the confusion.

What is without question is Caroline Dye's importance during her time, the widespread belief in her gift, and her lasting impact on American culture and blues music.

• LISTENING •

"St. Louis Blues" - Bessie Smith
"St. Louis Blues" - Cab Calloway
"St. Louis Blues" - Helen Humes
"Sundown Blues" - Daddy Stovepipe
"Aunt Caroline Dyer Blues" - Memphis Jug Band
"Hoodoo Woman" - Johnnie Temple
"Wang Dang Doodle" - Koko Taylor

DALE EVANS
Osceola

singer, actor, author, songwriter

A writer of iconic cowboy songs who became known as "Queen of the West," Frances Octavia Smith was born on Halloween 1912 in Texas and raised in Osceola.

She eloped and married at age 14 and had a son at age 15. Soon thereafter, she took business school courses. She found a secretarial job in Memphis, Tennessee, at a company that sponsored a radio program. She was singing at her desk when her boss overheard her and convinced her to appear on the radio show. Soon, Smith was a full-time vocalist on Memphis radio, divorced, and creating a music career as a single mother.

She changed her name from Frances Octavia Smith to the simpler Dale Evans when she took a job at WHAS in Louisville, Kentucky. In the late 1930s, she moved to Chicago, Illinois, and toured for a year with the Anson Weeks Orchestra. Afterward, she sang on CBS radio affiliate WBBM in Chicago for three years. Making the move to Hollywood, she shaved several years off her age and passed off son Tommy as her brother. She was briefly with 20th Century Fox Studios and sang on the Edgar Bergen and Charlie McCarthy show in 1942, then one of the most popular radio programs in the country. Around this time, Evans starred in musicals for Republic Pictures.

In 1944, the petite blonde was cast as the female lead in the film *The Cowboy And The Senorita* with the most popular movie cowboy of all time, Roy Rogers, then at his peak. Finding her niche, Evans began singing cowboy songs. They became a duo, professionally and personally. Evans and Rogers were married on New Year's Eve 1947. They starred in 19 more films together over the next five years.

Evans and Rogers eventually had nine children, fostering those with special needs. They had one shared biological child, Robin Elizabeth, who was born in 1950, diagnosed with Down syndrome, and died in 1952. The next year, Evans published *Angel Unaware*, a best-seller about how their family navigated Robin's life and death. The Happy Trails Children's Foundation carries on their work. Both Evans and Rogers were religious, and Evans wrote more than 20 books about her Christian faith.

A writer of songs as well as prose, Evans wrote "Happy Trails," which became the standard send-off for the couple's NBC television show, *The Roy Rogers Show*, which ran through the 1950s and cemented their stations in the American consciousness as icons of the West. Likewise, "Happy Trails" became an American classic, even

humorously covered by one of the most popular rock bands of the 1980s, Van Halen.

Evans also wrote the Christian chestnut "The Bible Tells Me So" and the Christmas song "The Story of Christmas," among others. Perhaps most enduring, however, are her interpretations with Rogers of Western-themed songs that became classics: "Home On The Range," "The Streets of Laredo," "Whoopee Ti Yi Yo," "Tumbling Tumbleweeds," "Cool Water," and "Bury Me Not On The Lone Prairie."

Frances "Dale Evans" Smith died of congestive heart failure on February 7, 2001, in Apple Valley, California, but still holds the title of "Queen of the West."

• LISTENING •

"The Bible Tells Me So" - Dale Evans and Roy Rogers
"Happy Trails" - Van Halen
"Cool Water" - Dale Evans and Roy Rogers
"The Streets of Laredo" - Dale Evans and Roy Rogers
"Home On The Range" - Dale Evans and Roy Rogers
"Whoopee Ti Yi Yo" - Dale Evans and Roy Rogers
"Tumbling Tumbleweeds" - Dale Evans and Roy Rogers

OLLIE GILBERT
Stone County

singer, musician, song collector

Ollie Gilbert was born Ollie Eva Woody in Hickory Grove on October 17, 1892. Although she was said to be a shy person, Gilbert became known among folklorists, festival audiences, and locals in North Central Arkansas for her jokes, banjo playing, ballad singing, and interest in song collecting.

She was the eighth of thirteen children. While still in single digits, young Ollie was playing a horsehair banjo made from a gourd with stretched squirrel hide. It was made by her brother, who felt bad for her that she didn't have a banjo. Spurred on by her mother's stories of the U.S. Civil War and the family's move West to Arkansas and Stone County, Ollie developed a love of history and of preserving and collecting old songs she'd hear, writing down the lyrics of songs that had largely been in the oral tradition. Ollie married Eual Oscar Gilbert before she'd turned 16. He was 24, a banjo player himself, a singer, and an alleged moonshiner. They had eight children.

Ollie Gilbert was said to have collected hundreds of songs. She was recorded by pioneering folklorists John Quincy Wolf Jr. and Max Hunter, and in October 1959, she was recorded in Timbo in her native Stone County by Alan Lomax and Shirley Collins. These folklorists, usually backed by their universities or the Library of Congress, would travel with heavy recording equipment into the hinterlands to record non-commercial singers and players, most often in their homes or the homes of friends, preserving many songs in the process that otherwise likely would have been lost.

One of the songs recorded by Lomax and Collins at that session was "It Rained A Mist," part of a body of ballads warning of children disappearing or being murdered by scary outsiders. Variants on this song date from the Middle Ages and can even be found in Chaucer's *Canterbury Tales*. It's just one of Gilbert's vast collection of songs, ballads, and saucy jokes, a list of which she kept on a long roll of cash register tape, according to folklorist W.K. McNeil.

Another of the songs she preserved, "Once I Courted A Lady Beauty Bright," is a song of parental confinement of their children. Not an uncommon topic of ballads of its era, in this song, the parents lock their child away from a potential suitor.

With the mid-20th century folk music resurgence, Gilbert became a nationwide festival attraction, performing, usually solo and a cappella, at concerts at the National Mall in Washington, D.C., New York, and the University of California, Los Angeles Folk Festival.

In the early 1960s, after Mountain View's Arkansas Folk Festival was revived very near where she was born, she became a regular performer there as well. She was recorded by Wolf and Hunter during the first year of the festival's revival in 1963. (Originally launched in 1941, the festival was halted with the U.S.'s entry into World War II.)

"When I retire, it'll be in the wooden box," Gilbert said to interviewer Studs Terkel in 1964 while in Chicago, Illinois, for a performance. Then in her 70s, she told him that she gardened every day.

A banjo player, song collector, and early member of the Rackensack Folklore Society, Ollie Eva Woody Gilbert—"Aunt Ollie"—died September 17, 1980. Buried at Timbo Cemetery in her native Stone County, she's a star among legends in that area of the state's incredible folk music legacy.

> • LISTENING •
> "It Rained A Mist" - Ollie Gilbert
> "Willow Green" - Ollie Gilbert
> "Lord Batesman" - Ollie Gilbert
> "Once I Courted A Lady Beauty Bright" - Ollie Gilbert
> "The Ballad of Cole Younger" - Ollie Gilbert
> "Pretty Polly Oliver" - Ollie Gilbert

BARBARA HENDRICKS
Stephens

opera and jazz vocalist, humanitarian

Barbara Hendricks of South Arkansas became one of North America's most acclaimed operatic voices as well as a humanitarian internationally recognized for her work with refugees.

Hendricks was born November 20, 1948, in Stephens. The daughter of a Methodist minister, Hendricks graduated with honors from Horace Mann High School in Little Rock and earned degrees in mathematics and chemistry. At the end of the 1960s, she switched gears and studied voice at the prestigious Julliard School of Music in New York.

Noted for her interpretations of French and Scandinavian composers over the usual German and Italian fare, the star of Barbara Hendricks rose quickly and internationally in the opera world. The soprano won competitions in New York, Switzerland, and France—all prior to her graduation from Julliard and her Paris recital debut in 1973. Hendricks's debut role was Susanna in *The Marriage of Figaro*. Her first recording was in 1974 as Clara in *Porgy and Bess*.

In the mid-1990s, she made the leap from singing opera to singing jazz. Typically, Hendricks went big. In 1994, she debuted at the Montreux Jazz Festival in Switzerland. She left her old record company, EMI, in 2006 and established her own label, Arte Verum. She's recorded exclusively for Arte Verum ever since.

While Hendricks was gaining notice musically, she was also gaining international attention for her endeavors outside of opera. In 1987, Hendricks was named an Ambassador of Goodwill for refugees by the United Nations. She played peace concerts in the former Yugoslavia in 1991 and 1993 and spoke at the fifth anniversary of the reunification of Germany in 1995. The native Arkansawyer was also named a Special Advisor on Interculturality by the Director General of UNESCO in 1994. Hendricks said she identified with the plight of refugees; growing up in segregated Arkansas, she often felt like a refugee in her own country.

She personalized her humanitarian work by founding the Barbara Hendricks Foundation for Peace and Reconciliation in 1998. This was the culmination of her years of work in war-torn areas around the globe and with refugees. In 2001, Hendricks performed at the

Nobel Peace Prize concert in Oslo, Norway. Her memoir, *Lifting My Voice* (Chicago Review Press, 2014), was translated into three languages.

A resident of Europe since the 1970s, this Swedish citizen, singer, and international humanitarian from small town Ouachita County could perhaps more accurately be called a citizen of the world.

• **LISTENING** •

"Die Forelle" - Barbara Hendricks
"Summertime" - Barbara Hendricks
"Vocalise En Forme de Habanera" - Barbara Hendricks
"Un Beldi" - Barbara Hendricks
"What A Little Moonlight Can Do" - Barbara Hendricks

VIOLET BRUMLEY HENSLEY
Montgomery County

fiddler, luthier

Violet Brumley was born October 21, 1916, near Mount Ida. She has become known worldwide for her fiddling, craft demonstrations, television appearances, instrument making, and wood carving—as well as her longevity, continuing her music and teaching well past the century mark. Called "The Stradivarius of the Ozarks," she nicknamed herself "The Whittling Fiddler."

Coming from a musical family, she began playing fiddle early in life, and as a teenager, made her first instrument. She apprenticed under her father, who had also made his first fiddle as a teen. She learned his techniques and used his largely 19th-century tool collection. She made four fiddles in the early 1930s.

At age 18, she married Adren Hensley. She continued playing music but put aside making fiddles for family life. After raising nine children, she returned to her craft in 1961, nearly 30 years later. She subsequently made dozens more, each taking hundreds of hours to complete.

The family moved to Yellville in Marion County in 1968, where she set up her work area for woodworking and repair. She used a variety of wood types for her instruments, including sassafras, pine, buckeye, cherry, and myrtle.

In addition to being a luthier, she's been a barber, blacksmith, and logger. But over her more than one hundred years of life, it's been fiddle playing and fiddle making that have captivated both her and her audiences.

She began as a craft presenter at Silver Dollar City a few years after the theme park's opening. She has since appeared on television shows ranging from *The Beverly Hillbillies* and *Captain Kangaroo* to *Live! with Regis and Kathy Lee*, and has done presentations at schools throughout the Midwest, most often wearing period costume and bonnet.

Brumley Hensley performed music with her family members, including with her husband until his death in 1997, and with her daughters, Lewonna and Sandra, and son, Calvin. Over the decades she, and they, have released a handful of recordings of classic old-time bluegrass songs such as "Boil Them Cabbage Down" and "Paddy Won't You Drink Some Cider?"

She has been featured in *National Geographic* magazine

and has given demonstrations and exhibits at festivals such as the Smithsonian Folklife Festival. Silver Dollar City gave her its Living Treasure Award in 1997, inducting her into its hall of fame. The Arkansas Arts Council named her an Arkansas Living Treasure in 2004, a designation reserved for those who elevate their work to the status of art and actively preserve and advance their art form through educating others.

She continued working on fiddles even as her eyesight failed, leaving the more detailed pieces to her apprentices.

Fresh off her induction into the National Fiddler Hall of Fame in Tulsa, Oklahoma, the previous month, she made her third appearance at The Grand Ole Opry in April 2018 at age 101.

On November 7, 2023, Violet Brumley Hensley celebrated her 107th birthday.

• **LISTENING** •

"Boil Them Cabbage Down" - Violet Hensley & Family
"Paddy Won't You Drink Some Cider?" - Violet Hensley & Family
"One-Eyed Gopher" - Yellville's Whittlin' Fiddler Violet Hensley
"Arkansas Traveler" - Yellville's Whittlin' Fiddler Violet Hensley
"Healthy Waltz" - Yellville's Whittlin' Fiddler Violet Hensley
"Train Whistle Blues" - Yellville's Whittlin' Fiddler Violet Hensley
"Walk Along John" - Yellville's Whittlin' Fiddler Violet Hensley

ZILPHIA HORTON
Logan County

musician, writer, arranger, activist

Zilphia Horton of Logan County became one of the most important musicians and song interpreters of the and mid-century U.S. labor and civil rights movements, helping crystallize the genre of freedom songs during a pivotal point in the country's history.

Horton was born Zilphia Mae Johnson in Paris on April 14, 1910. From a very young age, chestnut-haired Zilphia Mae took piano lessons. She later played guitar, accordion, and other instruments. The Logan County native studied to be a classical musician but instead is remembered for helping transform existing traditional songs like "We Shall Not Be Moved," "This Little Light of Mine," and "We Shall Overcome" into galvanizing anthems of the ongoing U.S. civil rights and labor movements—a folk subgenre often known as "freedom songs." Dr. Martin Luther King Jr. called freedom songs "the soul of the movement" and "as old as the history of the Negro in America."

With the state's coal deposits through West Central Arkansas, Logan County was a mining hub for decades. The Johnsons were a well-off family. Zilphia's father, Robert Guy, was a superintendent at the Paris Purity Coal Company. As Zilphia grew up, she stayed with music. Studying music and drama, she graduated from the Presbyterian-affiliated College of the Ozarks in nearby Clarksville in 1931.

Meanwhile, back in Paris, Rev. Claude Williams had become a preacher at Cumberland Presbyterian Church, which Zilphia attended. Rev. Williams had become known in the area for his sermons emphasizing Christ's teachings on helping the poor. Rev. Williams backed the unionization of the Purity Coal Company in 1934. So did most of his church congregation, including Zilphia. Zilphia's father, being with the coal company, did not.

In the wake of the family conflict over the coal strike, Zilphia went East to Tennessee's Highlander Folk School in early 1935. Myles Horton had founded the adult school a few years earlier. Highlander assisted U.S. labor unions in organizing in the 1930s and in the U.S. civil rights movement in the 1950s, and continues today. Just weeks after her arrival there, Zilphia and Myles Horton married. They had two children.

After the marriage, she reconciled with her father but forever continued her work to improve conditions for working people and to fight for justice and equality in

> Singer Lee Hays attended Cumberland Presbyterian Church in Paris, supported the coal strike, and attended College of the Ozarks with Zilphia Horton. Growing up the son of a Methodist preacher, Little Rock-born Hayes also lived in Paragould, Newport, and Booneville. Hays later sang bass with Pete Seeger and Woody Guthrie, and was part of the singing folk group The Weavers. He wrote songs like "If I Had A Hammer." Hays credited both Horton and Rev. Claude Williams with inspiring him to become a singer and to craft songs.

the U.S. She became the cultural director at the Highlander School, and her time there became her life's work, with her classes becoming legendary and attended by legends. Through the 1950s, Dr. Martin Luther King Jr., Rosa Parks, John Lewis, Fannie Lou Hamer, Stokely Carmichael, and other luminaries of the movement attended Highlander workshops.

As Highlander cultural director, Horton taught songwriting workshops, song collecting, and reworking and rewriting songs. She collected songs for an influential songbook published in 1939 for the United Textile Workers of America. She became a catalyst, putting together and teaching the songs that have motivated generations.

"This Little Light of Mine" is but one example. Besides its use at strikes, protests, and churches, the song has been performed onstage by artists ranging from Arkansawyer Rosetta Tharpe (see page 97) to Bruce Springsteen.

It has been used at such disparate events as Prince Harry and Meghan Markle's wedding in 2018, as well as by counter-protesters at the infamous Charlottesville, Virginia, white supremacist rally just a few months before.

Another, "We Shall Overcome," was an American slavery-era field song. South Carolina tobacco workers who had used the song in a 1945 strike brought it to Highlander School. Horton used it in her workshops, including teaching the song to famed folksinger Pete Seeger.

While 1901 sheet music has the title as "I'll Overcome Someday," the song's name was eventually tweaked from "I Will Overcome" to "We Shall Overcome." The song spread through the often overlapping causes of U.S. civil rights and U.S. labor rights to become an anthem of both. Joan Baez sang it at the 1963 March on Washington, D.C. President Lyndon Johnson repeated the phrase in his 1965 speech for voting rights. The phrase was invoked often by Dr. Martin Luther King Jr. including just days before his 1968 murder. Armed with that song, Congressman John Lewis said, "You were prepared to march into hell's fire."

"We Shall Not Be Moved" also dates to the slavery era in the U.S. Proving its power beyond its English-language origins, the song was translated for singing in Spanish, and a Swedish translation of the song played a part in anti-nuclear demonstrations in Sweden in the late 1970s. It's been recorded by everyone from jazz singer Ella Fitzgerald to Arkansas's Johnny Cash to rap group Public Enemy.

Folk and blues musician Huddie William "Leadbelly" Ledbetter said Horton was "the only white woman I know who could play Black music." She is also said to have inspired folk legend Woody Guthrie with the idea that songs could affect change.

Feeling that the piano put too much distance between herself and the other workshop participants, Horton played accordion and taught herself mountain dulcimer and recorder, adding to her classical training by immersing herself in folk music and hymns. However, Horton would use any era and type of music to get the message across—from Broadway tunes to popular music of the day, or hits from years before, songs from "Brother, Can You Spare A Dime?" to "Ac-Cent-Tchu-Ate The Positive."

To Horton, music and the arts were not dressing for political organizing, but essential tools in creating common cause and community, as illustrated by the endurance of the freedom songs she helped popularize.

Tragically, just days before her birthday on April 11, 1956, she died of poisoning from accidental ingestion of typewriter cleaning solution in Nashville, Tennessee.

A Singing Army, a biography of Horton by Kim Ruehl, was published in 2021 by the University of Texas Press. A testament to her legacy as a figure of renown in the music of social justice in the U.S. and internationally, Highlander School's Zilphia Horton Project continues decades after her death.

As Horton explained: "Music is not trimming! Music is the heart of things—of beliefs, of situations, of struggle, of ideas, of life itself."

• **LISTENING** •

"We Shall Overcome"
"We Shall Not Be Moved"
"This Little Light of Mine"
"Keep Your Eyes On The Prize"
"Woke Up This Morning With My Eyes On Freedom"
"Brother, Can You Spare A Dime?"

KENNI HUSKEY
Newport

musician, singer

Kenni Huskey became a pioneer in country music, despite never blazing the charts.

Huskey was born December 2, 1954, in Newport. The Huskeys were a musical family. Her father, Bill, moved the family to Memphis, Tennessee, to further his own rock 'n' roll dreams. He was a rockabilly performer in his own right during the Sun Records heyday. Later, her dad nurtured Kenni's talent, even writing for her and producing her early on.

She had her first paid gig when she was just 10, singing on Eddie Bond's *Country Shindig* show.

By the early 1960s, she was a veteran of the area club scene and Memphis television. In 1966, when she was just 13, she cut her first single, "Wild Man Tamer" / "Mister Future," written and produced by her dad Bill, and even performed at The Grand Ole Opry. The original was released on Jakebil Records, located on Dewey Avenue in Newport.

When the Huskeys moved West after her dad was transferred from Memphis, Tennessee, to Southern California, it only broadened the musical options for Kenni. She kept performing, and she and her dad became enamored with California's country "Bakersfield sound," and the most popular of its practitioners, Buck Owens, a native of Texas. Kenni was 15 when she was introduced to Owens, who was convinced by Kenni's dad to listen to her perform backstage before a benefit show. Owens liked what he heard, and within days, she was signed to Owens's label, Capitol Records.

Brandishing an acoustic guitar, Huskey played with Buck Owens's band, The Buckaroos, for five pivotal years in the 1970s, touring with the group and appearing on *The Buck Owens Ranch Show* on television as well as several episodes of *Hee Haw*.

On the Capitol label, Huskey continued recording country songs with sass and verve, like "Hollywood and Vine": "We left our home in Arkansas, you wanted to make good / So we moved out West to this old town they call Hollywood / Now we've been here for 13 weeks, but you ain't made a dime / Standing on the corner of Hollywood and Vine."

When she came of age, Huskey maintained her connections with Owens but branched out on her own. She moved to Nashville, Tennessee, and signed with another major record label, Warner Brothers. But marriage and a move to South Carolina, away from recording centers, stalled her career momentum.

In 2006, Huskey released an album titled *Tribute To My Second Dad … Buck Owens*. In 2010, her signature song, "Wild Man Tamer," was included on the Conway-based *Oxford American* magazine's 11th annual Southern Music CD.

No big hits and little radio airplay ever came to Huskey, despite the push from Owens and the major labels—and her own obvious star power. But Kenni "Wild Man Tamer" Huskey holds a special place in the hearts of fans of rockabilly and the Bakersfield sound.

> • **LISTENING** •
>
> "Mister Future" - Kenni Huskey
> "Wild Man Tamer" - Kenni Huskey
> "Hollywood & Vine" - Kenni Huskey
> "Number One Heel" - Buck Owens
> "Number One Heel" - Kenni Huskey
> "Tar & Cement" - Kenni Huskey
> "Living Tornado" - Kenni Huskey

MABLE JOHN
Ouachita County

vocalist, songwriter

Singer and writer Mable John was given the star treatment at two of the biggest Black record labels in the country, and for a dozen years, she sang with Ray Charles. But while her brother, Little Willie John, became an R&B star, Mable John found a higher purpose in life.

The oldest of ten children, John was born in Bastrop, Louisiana, near the Arkansas state line, on November 3, 1930. The Johns were a musical family, and the elder five children formed a gospel quintet. She was still an infant when the John family moved about a hundred miles Northwest to Cullendale. Her father, Mertis, was a logger, while her mother, Lillie, played guitar. Singing was decidedly encouraged around the John house.

"We weren't doing it to go into show business," John later recalled to author Rob Bowman. "We had fun as a family," she said. "It would be summertime, and we'd look out the windows and the people in the neighborhood would be all around our windows listening to us. We were just having fun. That's how we actually got into music." In 1942, just before she became a teenager, the family joined the wartime-era Great Migration for factory work in Detroit, Michigan. Her father got a job working on the automotive assembly line for Dodge. John's first job in Detroit was at Friendship Mutual, a life insurance company. It was given to her by Bertha Fuller Gordy—who happened to be the mother of Berry Gordy Jr., future Motown Records impresario. So when Bertha's son began looking for singing talent to fill the roster of his fledgling record company, originally called Tamla Records, John was a natural fit. She was the first woman signed to Tamla. Through the early 1960s, she released four singles. But eventually, John felt the label was too pop-oriented for her bluesy, low-register, smoky singing style. Although mentored and groomed by Gordy, she asked to be released from Motown's world of "Hitsville, U.S.A."

Meanwhile, Willie, one of John's brothers and a member of the family's early gospel group, became an R&B star in his own right through these years. Billed as Little Willie John, his 1956 recording of "Fever" became a smash that still resonates today. That same year, John toured with her brother's Little Willie John Revue, taking the place of Etta James. The two siblings appeared together at Harlem, New York's famed Apollo Theater in April 1960. Following her brother's tragic early death in prison in May 1968, John recorded a tribute version

MABLE JOHN

Little Willie John was born in 1937 in Cullendale, in Ouachita County, and became one of the greatest R&B singers of all time. Henry Glover of Hot Springs produced many hits on Willie John, including John's signature hit, "Fever," and "All Around The World," also known as "Grits Ain't Groceries," on Cincinnati, Ohio's King Records. Dropped from the King label in 1963, John was convicted of manslaughter two years later for stabbing a man in Seattle, Washington. Willie John died in prison at age 30 of an alleged heart attack in May 1968. James Brown released a Little Willie John tribute album later that year.

of Willie's 1956 hit "Need Your Love So Bad"—a song written by their brother Mertis Jr. for Willie.

In the mid-1960s, Brinkley-born Al Bell signed John to Stax Records, only weeks after he'd come to work at the Memphis, Tennessee, label. As she had at Motown, John was given the red carpet treatment at Stax, garnering songs written by the celebrated writing team of Isaac Hayes and David Porter, authors of such hits as "Hold On, I'm Coming," "Soul Man," and "When Something Is Wrong With My Baby." She also wrote much of her own material, as well as collaborating with Hayes and Porter, Steve Cropper, and other Stax luminaries.

John's studio bandmates were all aces too, including the aforementioned guitarist Cropper, keyboardist Booker T. Jones, drummer Al Jackson Jr., and trumpeter Wayne Jackson, a West Memphis native. Her background singers at Stax often included her brother Raymond, and members of Jeanne and the Darlings, a Little Rock group. But despite some regional successes, only her first single, "Your Good Thing Is About To End," saw any major national chart action, hitting #6 on the R&B charts.

Nicknamed "Able Mable" as a child by her mother, that also became one of her song titles (Ironically, "Able Mable" was musically similar to her brother Willie's signature song, "Fever"). Of her songs, which were often of heartache, she later told Bowman, "I've never recorded anything that was not a part of my own life."

In 1969, Ray Charles asked John if she knew anyone who would lead his group of backing female vocalists, The Raelettes. She said she didn't know anyone. But after months of pressure, Brother Ray convinced her *she* was the woman for the job. John would lead The Raelettes group for years. She was there as The Raelettes also became an act marketed separately from Charles, singing lead on the group's cover of "I Want To Do Everything For You" in 1970. Billed as "Ray Charles Presents The Raelettes," the group released its own full album on Charles's ill-fated Tangerine Records called *Yesterday … Today … Tomorrow*.

Despite her enduring songs and amazing players, inexplicably, John never became an R&B star in her own right. In the late 1970s, she became drawn to the ministry. She studied Greek and Hebrew in Israel and earned a doctorate in divinity in the early 1990s. And although she would still make sporadic appearances at music festivals and special concert events, she found a higher calling in distributing food and clothing to those in need in Southern California.

By the 1990s, John and her unjustly overlooked musical canon had begun getting its due. Most of her back catalog saw re-release on compilations, as well as her

first full solo album under her own name. In 1994, she received a Pioneer Award from the Rhythm and Blues Foundation.

John also pursued other artistic interests. In 2006, she co-authored a novel called *Sanctified Blues* (Random House) that told the suspiciously autobiographical story of a singer who became a spiritual leader. With David Ritz, she also authored additional titles based on her songs: *Love Tornado* and *Stay Out Of The Kitchen!* In 2007, art again mirrored life when she played a blues singer in the film *Honeydripper*, directed by John Sayles (*Eight Men Out, Sunshine State*). She also appeared in the Oscar-winning documentary film *20 Feet From Stardom*.

John died August 25, 2022, at age 91 in Los Angeles, California. Despite her lack of commercial success, Mable John remains a towering figure in R&B.

> • **LISTENING** •
>
> "Able Mable" - Mable John
> "Need Your Love So Bad" - Mable John
> "I'm A Big Girl Now" - Mable John
> "Stay Out Of The Kitchen" - Mable John
> "It's Catching" - Mable John
> "I Love You More Than Words Can Say" - Mable John
> "I Want To Do Everything For You" - The Raelettes
> "I Want To Do Everything For You" - Nazareth

MARJORIE LAWRENCE
Hot Springs

singer, teacher

A commanding voice in opera and an inspiring figure due to all she overcame, Marjorie Florence Lawrence was born February 17, 1907, in Deans Marsh, Victoria, Australia. Her father played fiddle; her mother was a church organist who died when Lawrence was only two years old. By age 10, Lawrence was singing solo and winning vocal competitions in Southern Australia. She first left her home for nearby Melbourne at age 18 to study voice. Following further voice studies in Paris, France, she debuted at Monte Carlo and, later, at the Paris Opera.

She debuted at New York's Metropolitan Opera House in 1935 and became known for the physicality of her performances. Of particular note was her 1936 role in Wagner's *Götterdämmerung*. During the finale, she jumped a horse through a ring of fire. Lawrence sang at the Met annually through the 1940 season, and she became an established figure in opera.

In summer of 1941, Lawrence collapsed while rehearsing in Mexico City, Mexico, and was diagnosed with polio. She and her osteopath husband moved to Hot Springs to work on her recovery. Lawrence received treatment at St. Joseph's Hospital and the Maurice Bathhouse. The couple settled down in Garland County and named their nearly 500-acre property "Harmony Hills."

Lawrence did recover, both physically and professionally. Her initial return to singing was on the radio the next year. In December 1942, Lawrence returned to New York's Met, singing the role of Venus from Wagner's *Tannhäuser* while sitting.

During World War II, she performed for thousands of soldiers, with special concerts for the wounded. In 1945, she toured Europe, including a performance at Buckingham Palace. By 1947, Lawrence was again able to stand while singing. Her health and career back on track, the couple remained in Arkansas.

An Oscar-winning 1955 film, *Interrupted Melody*, was based on Lawrence's 1949 autobiography of the same name. Eleanor Parker, who played Lawrence, was additionally nominated for an Oscar for her role. American soprano Eileen Farrell sang Parker's part in the film, which also starred Glenn Ford and Roger Moore, and premiered in Arkansas at the Malco Theatre in Hot Springs.

Lawrence hosted a television show sponsored by Coca-Cola in the mid-1950s. She also began teaching and doing voice and opera workshops at Tulane University in New Orleans, Louisiana, and Southern Illinois University in Carbondale.

During summers, Lawrence conducted voice workshops at her home in Hot Springs, nurturing new opera talent in the state.

She began teaching at Garland County Community College in Hot Springs in 1974 and joined the faculty of the University of Arkansas at Little Rock the following year.

Some of Lawrence's best-known roles were Salome, Tosca, and Carmen. But as a native Australian, her signature song, fittingly, was "Waltzing Matilda," which she recorded several times, also including it among her final recording sessions in 1976.

Marjorie Lawrence, an adopted Arkansawyer and an inspiration, died January 13, 1979, at St. Vincent Hospital in Little Rock and is buried in Greenwood Cemetery in Hot Springs.

• LISTENING •

Tannhäuser - Marjorie Lawrence
"Waltzing Matilda" - Marjorie Lawrence
Götterdämmerung - Marjorie Lawrence
Die Walküre - Marjorie Lawrence

KETTY LESTER
Hope

vocalist, actress

Ketty Lester became known internationally as a chanteuse and an actress, much of her notoriety on the strength of one hit song—but what a song it was. Her haunting version of the lasting pop song "Love Letters" and the name Ketty Lester will be forever intertwined.

Lester was born Revoyda Frierson in Hope on August 16, 1934. Revoyda was one of 15 children and the granddaughter of enslaved people. The Friersons were a farming family in Hempstead County. Even as a child, she sang, particularly at school and in church choirs, and she also loved play-acting.

After turning down a music scholarship from Philander Smith College in Little Rock, Frierson relocated at age 17 to San Francisco, California, to study nursing on a scholarship at San Francisco City College. But she maintained her theatrical and musical side and got gigs singing in area nightclubs. It was around this time that she took on the stage name Ketty Lester in lieu of the more cumbersome Revoyda Frierson.

But eventually for Lester, the lure of performing—coupled with an aversion to human cadavers—won out over the nursing profession. As she laughingly explained to Groucho Marx on television's *You Bet Your Life* in 1957, "I just did all right until I got to anatomy. I walked in there one day and they had this dead man laying out there, and the [instructor] said, 'Ms. Frierson, would you come up and cut out the torso muscle?' And I said, 'What did you say? Are you kidding?' … And he said, 'How do you expect to finish this course if you don't cooperate?' And I said, 'Who is not cooperating? It's this poor sap here who's not cooperating!'"

Marx opined after hearing her sing that Lester was "going to be one of our top stars before long." And, less than five years later, Groucho was right.

Her first recording contract was with Everest Records of New York. However, her initial single, "Queen For a Day," tanked. She subsequently signed with Era Records of Los Angeles, California, in 1961. Her first release for Era was "Love Letters" in early 1962. It became a million-seller and an evergreen song well beyond Lester's version. Her *Love Letters* album was nominated for a Grammy, and she toured the United Kingdom opening for The Everly Brothers. Since then, the song "Love Letters" has been recorded by hundreds of artists over the decades, including Elvis Presley, Tony Bennett, and

Rosemary Clooney—musicians ranging from crooner Perry Como to former Sex Pistol Steve Jones.

Lester's relaxed, breathy vocal delivery was perfect for the song's aching lyrics, describing the thrill of receiving a letter from a faraway loved one: "Love letters straight from your heart / Keep us so near while apart / . . . I'm not alone in the night / When I can have all the love you write / I memorize every line / I kiss the name you sign."

This version of "Love Letters"—a spare, slow, melancholic arrangement with jazz great Earl Palmer on drums—reached the top five in the U.S. It fared just as well as in the U.K. and beyond, becoming a truly international pop hit.

Lester later recorded for RCA in 1964 and for Capitol Records in 1966. And while she was never able to again match the runaway commercial success of "Love Letters," the ubiquity of her most notable song surely widened the gateway into the other forms of entertainment she then pursued.

Statuesque and widely recognized for her beauty, Lester diversified into her other childhood love—acting—through the mid-1960s. She continued singing but also began making guest appearances on such notable television series of the late 1960s and 1970s as *Love, American Style*; *Room 222*; *Marcus Welby, M.D.*; *Laugh-In*; *That Girl*; *Green Acres*; *The Waltons*; and *Happy Days*. In the 1980s, she could be seen on *Webster*; *What's Happening Now!*; *L.A. Law*; *Hill Street Blues*; and *St. Elsewhere*. One of her most notable guest turns on television was a 1973 episode of *Sanford and Son* where Lester played a woman who had dated both Sanford and son. In 1998, she played Nana, the grandmother in the short-lived Vivica Fox sitcom *Getting Personal*.

In the mid-1970s, Lester was a regular on the long-running soap opera *Days of Our Lives*, playing the character Helen Grant. For five years, she played Hester-Sue Terhune on television's *Little House On The Prairie*, who taught at the blind school and waitressed at Nellie's, appearing in dozens of episodes of the series. In both instances, with African American television actors often excluded from meatier roles, Lester provided important Black representation.

Sylvia Dee was a writer and song lyricist born Josephine Desylvia Moore in 1914 in Little Rock. Dee also wrote short stories, Broadway stage scores, and such songs as "The End of the World," "Too Young," "Bring Me Sunshine," and others.

Lester's supporting acting in movies includes some of the best-known Black films of the era. They've run the gamut from her portrayal of Alma in 1968's *Up Tight*, probably her best-reviewed film, to her turn as Aunt Lucy in 1994's *House Party 3*. Film critic Roger Ebert favorably noted that *Up Tight* "had nerve enough to portray the anger of the ghetto."

Lester also played Juanita Jones, the cab driver-turned-vampire, in 1972's *Blacula*, considered the first horror so-termed "blaxsploitation" movie. She also played the character Irma Franklin in 1974's *Uptown Saturday Night*, starring Harry Belafonte and Sidney Poitier and directed by Poitier.

Meanwhile, the 1970s and 1980s saw her musical releases slow to a bare trickle and eventually stop. However, in

1984, returning to her Arkansas childhood roots, Lester recorded an album of Christian gospel music.

But beyond her acting—and even beyond a legendary song like "Love Letters"—Lester's other recordings have maintained an enduring appeal. Lester's song "Look For Me, I'll Be Around," co-written by Little Rock native Sylvia Dee, was recorded by Sarah Vaughan and revived by singer Neko Case in 2002.

Lester's unique low vocal range and classic song choices have made her a favorite of vinyl crate diggers and fans of vintage mid-century pop—although she did record a few less-obvious titles, such as a peppy version of the Woody Guthrie folk classic, "This Land Is Your Land."

A resident of Los Angeles, California, for years, Lester recalled her early days in her home state with the 2020 release of her memoir from Elite Publishing House, *Ketty Lester: From Arkansas To Grammy-Nominated 'Love Letters' to Little House on the Prairie*.

• **LISTENING** •

"Love Letters" - Ketty Lester
"But Not For Me" - Ketty Lester
"Sweet Torture" - Ketty Lester
"This Land Is Your Land" - Ketty Lester
"Look For Me, I'll Be Around" - Ketty Lester
"Love Letters" - Joe Walsh
"Love Letters" - Steve Jones
"Love Letters" - Rosemary Clooney
"Look For Me, I'll Be Around" - Neko Case

ROBERTA MARTIN
Helena

gospel singer, composer, music publisher

Although she trained as a classical concert pianist, Roberta Martin became a giant in gospel music as a choir director, performer, and music publisher during gospel's mid-20th century U.S. commercial heyday.

She was born Roberta Evelyn Winston on February 12, 1907, in Helena. One of six children, she was playing piano at a young age.

The Winstons moved from Phillips County to Cairo, Illinois. Eventually, Roberta landed in Chicago, where she would become highly influential in the city's huge gospel music scene as a performer, pianist, arranger, choral director, and, perhaps most notably, as a music publisher.

In the early 1930s, she formed The Martin-Frye Quartet with Theodore Frye; she changed its name to The Roberta Martin Singers in 1936. The group had an ever-changing lineup of some of the best young gospel singers in Chicagoland. Martin led the group, played piano, and directed the singers, but, despite the name, only occasionally took a vocal solo turn herself. She'd married Bill Martin and continued using the name Martin as her stage name even after their divorce and her subsequent marriage to James Austin in 1947. Her trademark was allowing distinct individual voices to be heard within the harmony despite being in group choral settings, giving more immediacy and intensity to the gospel message. In the 1940s, The Roberta Martin Singers became one of the biggest names in Black gospel music.

However, equally important in her career—as well as to the musical careers of others—was Martin's role as a music publisher. As a long-term source of income, the importance of controlling one's publishing can scarcely be underestimated in an artist's career, and Martin fulfilled that role. Her publishing house, the Roberta Martin Studio of Music, launched in 1939, just as her career was taking off. Controlling her own publishing allowed Martin to better control her income and thus better control her destiny, as well as that of other artists. Her song "Try Jesus, He Satisfies" has particularly been a perennial favorite, recorded by many gospel singers, and featured in hymnals. The Martin publishing house handled Martin's own compositions as well as those of other gospel songwriters, such as James Cleveland.

She died January 18, 1969, in Chicago, Illinois. Thousands of mourners attended her funeral. Nearly thirty years after Martin's death, the U.S. Postal Service featured her on a postage stamp in 1998. Roberta Martin's legacies in choral gospel and music publishing still echo.

• LISTENING •

"Only A Look" - The Roberta Martin Singers Of Chicago
"I Have Hope" - Roberta Martin
"Just Jesus And Me" - The Roberta Martin Singers
"He Knows How Much We Can Bear" - The Roberta Martin Singers
"Try Jesus, He Satisfies" - Velma Moore
"God Is Still On The Throne" - The Bright Stars
"God Specializes" - The Roberta Martin Singers

ROSE MARIE MCCOY
Oneida

songwriter, performer

Pioneering songwriter Rose Marie McCoy was born Marie Hinton on April 19, 1922, in tiny Oneida in Phillips County, where her parents farmed. The family was poor. She attended Eliza Miller High School in nearby Helena, where she lived with her grandparents. The Eliza Miller High School was begun by the businesswoman and educator Eliza Miller, who was an Arkadelphia native. Opening in 1926, it was the first high school for Black students in Phillips County, and it later hosted musical acts such as B.B. King. Being in Helena, home to so many performers, McCoy learned to love the blues herself.

By the time she was out of her teens, Hinton had moved to New York City to make it as a singer and legally added "Rose" to her name. She married childhood sweetheart James McCoy on a trip back home to Arkansas in 1943 before James was transferred overseas for World War II. (They had no children, and he died in 2000.) Based in New York, she opened up for the likes of groundbreaking Black comedians Pigmeat Markham and Moms Mabley, as well as singers Dinah Washington and Ruth Brown.

Although she also tried to make it as a performer, it was songwriting, not singing, that would prove to be McCoy's greatest gift to American popular music. In 1946, the gospel vocal quartet The Dixieaires was the first to record a McCoy song, but it was the early 1950s before McCoy saw her first real chart success: "Gabbin' Blues" by Big Maybelle, which reached number three on the R&B chart in 1953.

From there, McCoy wrote songs recorded by Big Joe Turner, Nat King Cole, Sarah Vaughn, The Drifters, and such fellow Arkansas artists as Al Hibbler, Louis Jordan, and Little Willie John—all giants in R&B and jazz music. McCoy wrote several songs with Willie John's producer, Hot Springs native Henry Glover. This includes Little Willie John's "Uh Uh Baby" and "If I Thought You Needed Me."

Elvis Presley's version of the McCoy song "Tryin' To Get To You" was released on Presley's 1956 debut album. It was subsequently recorded by Roy Orbison, Ricky Nelson, and, later, by Eric Burdon, Johnny Rivers, and Faith Hill, among others.

"Thank god for Elvis," McCoy would later say, although she wasn't a big fan of his version of her song. In 1958,

Presley recorded McCoy's song "I Beg of You," which hit the top ten as the B-side of Presley's single, "Don't."

Brinkley native and R&B pioneer Louis Jordan recorded McCoy's aching blues "If I Had Any Sense, I'd Go Back Home" in the mid-1950s when his career was faltering after a decade of wild success, singing: "I realized fortune and fame is not for me, and all those pretty stories ain't what they're cooked up to be . . . ." And while the song may have seemed autobiographical to Jordan, McCoy was having the same self-doubt when she wrote it.

But the Arkansawyer needn't have worried about her musical legacy, even as it has only recently gained more widespread attention. McCoy was still just getting started then, and she continued to have hit songs through the genres and the years, primarily in R&B and jazz, but also in rock, pop, gospel, and country music. Hundreds of artists have recorded Rose Marie McCoy songs.

Over the years, McCoy won seven BMI songwriting awards. Ike and Tina Turner's 1961 version of McCoy's song "It's Gonna Work Out Fine" was nominated for a Grammy. McCoy was inducted into the Arkansas Black Hall of Fame in 2008, and in June 2018, she was inducted into the Arkansas Jazz Hall of Fame.

Arlene Corsano of New Jersey wrote a biography of McCoy called *Thought We Were Writing the Blues, But They Called It Rock 'N' Roll* (ArleneCristine, 2014). Just months after its publication, on January 20, 2015, Rose Marie McCoy died at the age of 92, a giant in songwriting across genres.

"I don't know of any other songwriter with the kind of track record Rose Marie McCoy has," Brinkley native and legendary record producer Al Bell said of her work: "Her songs have been recorded by so many legendary artists in such a diversity of styles. It's mind-boggling what she has done."

• **LISTENING** •

"Gabbin' Blues" - Big Maybelle
"It's Gonna Work Out Fine" - Ike & Tina Turner
"Uh Uh Baby" - Little Willie John
"Letter From My Darling" - Little Willie John
"If I Had Any Sense, I'd Go Back Home" - Louis Jordan
"House Party" - Louis Jordan
"I Beg Of You" - Elvis Presley

PATSY MONTANA
Garland County / Hope

musician, singer, actor

Patsy Montana, born Rubye Rebecca Blevins on October 30, 1908, became the first female million-selling artist in the history of country music.

The Blevins family came from the Ozarks, homesteaded in Mena, and moved to Jessieville when Rubye was two. Her father, Augustus, born in Howard County, taught school and sang in church. Her mother, Victoria, from Pike County, played the organ and was Jessieville's postmistress. The family home doubled as the post office. "Actually, Daddy was [officially] the postmaster for our little community, because women could not hold that title," Montana noted in her autobiography, published in 2002, six years after her death. A couple of years later, the family moved to Hope when transferred by the postal service.

"From a very early age, I had music around me almost every waking minute, and it ranged from opera to a Black man's blues," Montana said. A rough-and-tumble type raised with only male siblings, she learned to play the fiddle after a brother acquired one, eventually competing around Hempstead County.

At age 14, Montana and her brother performed at the dedication of an area bridge and were paid the then-handsome sum of five dollars. However, her guitar-playing sibling thought he deserved more than half the take. "It did not seem fair to him at all," she said, "but I stuck to my guns. In the end, the 50-50 split is all he got. At that moment, I started women's lib in Arkansas."

In 1930, Montana moved to California with her older brother to study classical violin at University of California, Los Angeles. She ended up dropping out after winning a talent contest by singing Jimmie Rodgers songs. By 1932, she was known professionally as Patsy Montana.

The next year, while taking Hope watermelons to the Chicago World's Fair, she visited the city's radio station WLS and ended up staying 15 years as vocalist for the Prairie Ramblers on the famed station's *National Barn Dance*. In August 1935, at the 26-year-old's first major recording session, Montana recorded her signature song: "I Want To Be A Cowboy's Sweetheart." It became the first song by a female country artist to sell a million copies.

Montana was a talented vocalist, guitarist, writer, and

fiddler. She also tried acting. In 1939, she appeared in the Gene Autry movie *Colorado Sunset*. In 1948, Montana returned to her native Southwest Arkansas, settling in Hot Springs with her two daughters and appearing on the Spa City's KTHS radio station (see page 41). In 1952, she returned to California.

Montana never again matched the chart success of "I Want To Be A Cowboy's Sweetheart," but the song lost little of its luster for her audiences over the years—or for other performers: Suzy Bogguss, The Chicks, and LeAnn Rimes are among those who have covered "I Want To Be A Cowboy's Sweetheart."

Rubye "Patsy Montana" Blevins, "The Cowboy's Sweetheart" died May 3, 1996. The same year, she was inducted into the Country Music Hall of Fame.

• LISTENING •

"The She Buckaroo" - Patsy Montana
"I Want To Be A Cowboy's Sweetheart" - Patsy Montana
"The Moon Hangs Low (On The Ohio)" - Patsy Montana
"Little Sweetheart of the Ozarks" - Patsy Montana
"My Million Dollar Smile" - Patsy Montana
"Ridin' Old Paint" - Patsy Montana

K.T. OSLIN
Crossett

songwriter, performer

K.T. Oslin was a country music pioneer whose time on top was short, but who had a lasting impact.

Future Nashville Songwriters Hall of Famer and multiple Grammy winner Oslin was born Kay Toinette Oslin on May 15, 1942, in Crossett, which was founded as a lumber town. Her father, Larry, worked as a foreman at the paper mill, but died of leukemia when Kay was only five years old. Her mother, Kathleen Byrd Oslin, worked for Veterans Affairs. Oslin also lived in Memphis, Tennessee, and Houston, Texas, where the family moved after her father's death. Growing up, Kay's role models were her mother and grandmother—the kind of strong, independent women who would often populate Kay's songs as an adult.

Oslin attended Lon Morris College, a Methodist-affiliated private college in Jacksonville, Texas, and majored in drama. In addition to her theatrical aspirations, she also got into folk music, which was enjoying a resurgence in popularity and was often heard on U.S. college campuses. Oslin was in a folk trio with Guy Clark, a musician who became—like Oslin—a Grammy-winning country music songwriting legend. The trio even recorded an album, but it went nowhere, despite Oslin and Clark's combined future star power. Clark got a solo record deal in the mid-1970s, and his songs were recorded by Johnny Cash, Willie Nelson, Jimmy Buffett, and many others.

In the mid-1960s, eager to give her college major studies a try, Oslin moved to New York City to pursue a career in acting. She ended up living there for 20 years, working steadily. Oslin appeared on and off Broadway in *Promises, Promises*; *Hello, Dolly!*; *West Side Story*; and other lesser-known productions. Besides performing onstage, Oslin could often be seen on television, singing jingles and acting in commercials for hemorrhoid creams, soft drinks, denture creams, cleaning products, and the like.

But music remained on Oslin's mind—and not just the music from a television jingle. In the early 1980s, she released a couple of country-sounding singles as "Kay T. Oslin," on Elektra—a record label never known for country music. After they sank commercially, she asked to be released from her recording contract. But Oslin's songs—with titles like "Clean Your Own Tables" and "Younger Men (Are Starting To Catch My Eye)"—stood out. After twenty years of pursuing a different type of show business success, it was Oslin's skills as a songwriter that created her unlikely country music breakthrough in middle age. Oslin was in her mid 40s when her debut album, *80's Ladies*, was released by RCA Records.

The 1987 album was a huge smash, launching her immediately onto country music's A-list. *80's Ladies* became a country music juggernaut, as did Oslin, who by then was going professionally as K.T. "I thought [this album] was my last chance at doing anything in this business, which was all that I knew how to do," the Ashley County native told *Billboard* magazine in 2015.

With her background, Oslin's lyrics nimbly addressed issues rarely heard in country music, touching on sexism and ageism in life and love. And there was an audience for what Oslin had to say, even beyond her own voice. In addition to her incredibly successful solo career, Oslin's songs have been recorded by such country music legends as Dottie West, Gail Davies, Dusty Springfield, and The Judds. Despite being launched as a "new" artist at 45, Oslin was embraced by the music industry's establishment. In the decades since Oslin's brief reign at the top, country artists have only continued to skew younger.

80's Ladies was eventually certified platinum. The album's hit title song earned Oslin the Country Music Association Award for Song of the Year, the first-ever female songwriter to win the award. "Do Ya" from the album became her first number one song. At an age when many singers are planning their comebacks, Oslin won a Grammy and was named CMA Female Vocalist of the Year.

Although her later-in-life debut was nearly singular in its vision, Oslin proved it was not an anomaly. The follow-up to *80's Ladies*, 1988's *This Woman*, continued the thread of her keyboard-driven, sometimes sad, often sardonic laments of grown-up love and adulthood complications. Like *80's Ladies*, *This Woman* also went platinum, also won a CMA Award, and, this time, added two Grammys to Oslin's collection.

Songwriting "gives me control, and gives me a way of expressing something that I would do uniquely," Oslin told television's *CBS This Morning* in 1990. "I ain't young, and I ain't pretty, and I ain't the most fabulous singer in the world," she said, "but I can put across my own thoughts and music in a way that nobody else can. So that's what makes it work."

Her third album, 1990's *Love In A Small Town*, hit the top five and was certified gold. It included her biggest hit, "Come Next Monday." Oslin toured as if she were making up for lost time—which she was. Displaying her theatrical roots, she often appeared onstage wearing opera gloves, coyly fanning an accordion fan around her face.

With only three albums to her credit—but several hit songs, including four number ones—Oslin released a greatest hits album: 1993's wonderfully-titled *Songs From An Aging Sex Bomb*. Then, she retired from music and the road. "The [music] business started changing very rapidly there, about my third or fourth year into my [record] deal," she told *Billboard* in 2015. "It got younger and younger, and I didn't want to fight it," she said. ". . . So I asked my business people if I had enough money to quit. And they said I did. So that's what I did." She would release music and make concert appearances only sporadically for the rest of her career.

Oslin then did some acting, including in the Sandra Bullock-starring 1993 film *The Thing Called Love* and an

episode of *The Carol Burnett Show*. She made a one-off appearance on the Sharp County, Arkansas-based *Evening Shade*, a sitcom produced by Hampton native Harry Thomason and Linda Bloodworth-Thomason of Poplar Bluff, Missouri. With Oslin's notably mature lyrical worldview, sense of self-deprecating humor, and unique backstory, she was also a sought-after guest for television profiles and talk shows—no longer the actor pitching denture cream between segments.

In 1996, only a year after she'd undergone quadruple bypass surgery, Oslin released a new album, *My Roots Are Showing*. Then, another five years passed before her next one, *Live Close By, Visit Often*.

Oslin's final album was also her first in 14 years and only her sixth over a country music career that spanned four decades. Called *Simply*, it was released in 2015. The same year, she was diagnosed with Parkinson's disease. She moved into assisted living in 2016. *Simply* included a reworking of "80's Ladies," bringing her recording career full circle. More than any other single Oslin song, "80's Ladies" was the one that had started it all for her, the title song of the album that had launched her into country music stardom in the second half of her life. "I still love that song," she said in 2015. "I don't know how I managed to write it, but it was a great song."

Oslin died December 21, 2020, at 78. She'd been diagnosed with covid just a week prior to her death. K.T. Oslin is remembered for her all-too-unique songwriting voice in country music and her reminder that midlife is as good a time as any to launch a career.

• **LISTENING** •

"Clean Your Own Tables" - K.T. Oslin
"Younger Men" - K.T. Oslin
"Do Ya'" - K.T. Oslin
"Didn't Expect It To Go Down This Way"- K.T. Oslin
"80's Ladies" - K.T. Oslin
"Hey Bobby" - K.T. Oslin
"Come Next Monday" - K.T. Oslin

FLORENCE PRICE
Little Rock

composer, performer

Florence Price was a groundbreaking composer, performer, and teacher.

She was born Florence Beatrice Smith on April 9, 1887, in Little Rock. Her mother, also named Florence, taught piano. Her father was a dentist. Interested in music from an early age, young Florence learned from her mother and published musical pieces while still in high school. She graduated from Little Rock's Capitol Hill School in 1903 as class valedictorian.

After studying at Boston, Massachusetts's New England Conservatory of Music and receiving degrees, Price concentrated on teaching. She taught in Cotton Plant and at Shorter College in North Little Rock and headed the music department at Atlanta, Georgia's Clark University before returning to Little Rock to marry attorney Thomas Jewell Price. (Thomas Price was on the legal team that won the freedom of the defendants in the 1919 race massacre in Elaine. Florence and Thomas had three children and divorced in 1931.)

In Arkansas's capital city, she taught students piano and continued composing. But Price found advancement difficult in her hometown because she was Black, even being refused membership in the Arkansas State Music Teachers Association due to her race. In 1927, the couple moved to Chicago, Illinois, and Price continued teaching and playing, becoming a leader in the city's musical community and also coming into her own as a composer.

The next year, she published four piano pieces. Her "Symphony No. 1 In E Minor" debuted with the Chicago Symphony Orchestra in 1933, making her piece the first by a female African American composer to be played by a major orchestra in the United States. Through the 1930s and 1940s, other orchestras in U.S. and European cities followed suit in performing her works. Price stood alone as a Black female classical composer working at the international level.

In 1935, Price made a triumphant homecoming, performing a concert of her works at Little Rock's racially segregated Black high school, Dunbar High.

A composer of hundreds of varied works—chamber music, choral works, solo works, symphonies, concertos, and more—Florence Price died June 3, 1953, in Chicago. But her story did not end then. In 2009, Price's manuscripts and papers were discovered in her former home, causing a renewed appreciation of her career.

> • **LISTENING** •
>
> "Arkansas Jitter" - Florence Price
> "Symphony No. 1 In E Minor" - Florence Price
> "Dance Of The Cotton Blossoms" - Florence Price
> "Concerto In One Movement" - Florence Price
> "Song To The Dark Virgin" - Florence Price
> "Violin Concerto No. 2" - Florence Price

ALMEDA RIDDLE
Cleburne County / White County

song collector, singer

Revered folk songster Almeda Riddle was seemingly made to be an Ozark song collector, saving hundreds of old ballads from being lost. She was born Almeda James on November 21, 1898, in the Cleburne County community of West Pangburn. She was educated by her parents, who were musical. Riddle would later say her father taught her to read music even before she could read words.

Even as a child, she collected songs—particularly after her father became a grocer near the local railroad station. There, she met people and heard songs from backgrounds beyond her native North Central Arkansas. Her practice of ballad collecting continued after she married H. Price Riddle in 1916 while she was still a teenager.

Ten years later, however, a tornado killed her husband and their youngest child. Riddle's thick book of the ballads she had been collecting for years also was lost. But Riddle was undaunted by the tragedy. She carried on, raising her remaining three children as a single mother, all while refilling her legendary songbook.

In the early 1950s, interest in American folk music was on the rise. A neighbor introduced Riddle to John Quincy Wolf Jr., an instructor in the emerging field of folklore study. A native of Batesville, Wolf taught at Southwestern College in Memphis, Tennessee, now known as Rhodes College. He was amazed by her collection of songs, some of which were centuries old, brought to the continent by early European settlers.

Wolf recommended Riddle to Alan Lomax, who is now considered the U.S.'s landmark ethnomusicologist. In October 1959, Lomax and Shirley Collins recorded Riddle in Greers Ferry. During this visit, Lomax recorded several others from the region as well, on the suggestion of Wolf and Stone County native Jimmie Driftwood.

Riddle recorded several songs for the folklorists that October. "Bury Me Beneath the Willow" was likely composed in the second half of the 19th century and was recorded by the Carter Family in the 1930s.

Riddle's "Merry Golden Tree" is a tragic tale of a lad who heroically sinks an enemy pirate ship, only to be duped by his own captain. The ballad dates from the 1700s, and was lyrically altered by Riddle and previous singers, a practice said to be more common among Ozark songsters than their counterparts elsewhere.

> Jimmie Driftwood of Timbo rode the folk music wave to stardom during this era with songs like "The Battle of New Orleans," which won him a Grammy at the second-ever Grammy Awards in 1959. Driftwood's other signature hit, "Tennessee Stud," was about an actual Arkansas racehorse. Driftwood's musician father, Neil Morris, was among those captured on tape at these fall 1959 field sessions, where Morris quoted his father and uncle, both music teachers, saying "that music had no end. . . . They said that music grew like the grapevine that is never pruned, that each year it put on a little bit more. That is what they said about it. Any further questions?"

Riddle also was recorded singing "Down in Arkansas," a comic ballad: "She is cross-eyed, that's a fact, but she's down in Arkansas / She cries and the tears rolls down her back, but she's down in Arkansas." Corny jokes abound in the song, which dates from territorial times, with the lines all ending with "down in Arkansas." In another verse, "She was cutting hay while the north wind blows / The sickle slipped and it cut off her nose / Doctor put it on, but upside down / Now when it rains she almost drowns, down in Arkansas."

Riddle wore long dresses onstage, sometimes with a bonnet over her curly tresses, and almost always sang a cappella. Despite her lifelong devotion to songs and her many performances, she did not consider herself an entertainer or performer. She often said, "A singer should not get in the way of a song, but just stand back."

She was a stickler for the ballad form, which originated in the Middle Ages and continued even with European settlement in North America. She recorded hundreds of songs.

Through her later years, she traveled the nation, singing her ballads at concerts, conferences, and seminars at Yale University, Harvard University, the University of California, Los Angeles, and in Washington, D.C., and beyond. For her contributions to Ozark folksong traditions, she was given the National Heritage Award from the National Endowment for the Arts and was the subject of a half-hour television documentary film. Her final performance in her home state was at Mountain View's Ozark Folk Center in 1984.

Affectionately known as "Granny Riddle," she lived her life in Cleburne and White counties, but spent a lifetime educating the country's academia with her deep knowledge of antiquated songs that might have otherwise been lost to history.

Riddle died on June 30, 1986, in Heber Springs, with no full count on the number of "old songs" she preserved, or the number of lives she influenced. Her goal to save as many historic ballads as possible for upcoming generations—or, "getting out the old songs"—however, was surely fulfilled.

• LISTENING •

"Down In Arkansas" - Almeda Riddle
"Bury Me Beneath The Willow" - Almeda Riddle
"Merry Golden Tree" - Almeda Riddle
"I Love My Little Rooster" - Almeda Riddle
"Poor Wayfaring Stranger" - Almeda Riddle
"Go Tell Aunt Nancy" - Almeda Riddle
"The House Carpenter" - Almeda Riddle

ROSETTA THARPE
Cotton Plant

guitarist, singer

A pioneer of guitar technique and a blender of genres, Sister Rosetta Tharpe was born Rosetta Nubin (possibly Atkins or Atkinson) on March 20, 1915, in Cotton Plant.

Tharpe's next-level guitar skills and singing voice first gained her attention in the Pentecostal Christian Church Of God In Christ, the church denomination in which she was raised, often performing with her Dallas County-born, evangelical, mandolin-playing, singing mother Katie Bell Nubin (Harper)—or "Mother Nubin" to her daughter's "Sister Rosetta." At age four, Rosetta began performing, and by age six appeared regularly with her mother.

Perhaps due to her singular talents, Tharpe rose up quickly in the gospel music ranks through the 1930s. Her voice was notable, but her guitar skills were extraordinary; her tones, melodies, and riffs unlike any other before her. She signed to Decca Records in 1938 and began to appeal to wider, more secular audiences. She even recorded some secular music, much to the chagrin of the church.

Author of the first biography written on Tharpe, *Shout, Sister, Shout!: The Untold Story of Rock 'N' Roll Trailblazer Sister Rosetta Tharpe* (Beacon Press, 2007), Gayle Wald told *Arkansongs* that Tharpe "dared to defy the conventions of the community that nourished her musical talent. Publicly, she was never cowed by [church] pressure. She was a remarkable woman for daring to make her music in the way that she wanted to make it."

Among her secular musical pursuits, Tharpe performed and recorded with Cab Calloway, Duke Ellington, and her Decca Records label mates Louis Jordan of Brinkley, and Lucky Millinder and His Orchestra. Millinder's band included Hot Springs native Henry Glover, later an esteemed songwriter and producer. With Millinder, Tharpe recorded 1942's scandalously-titled, definitely non-gospel song "I Want A Tall Skinny Papa." Tharpe, Millinder, and Millinder's band even shot a short film, among the early examples of promotional "music video," for the song.

She married C.O.G.I.C. pastor Thomas Thorpe as a teenager. Later in the 1940s, she married music promoter Fosh Allen. But she used the "Tharpe" name variation as her professional surname for the rest of her life, and had relationships with both women and men. Her third marriage was her most extravagant. In July 1951, Tharpe married Russell Morrison in front of a packed crowd at Griffith Stadium, home of baseball's Washington Senators, charging as much as $2.50 per ticket, and later releasing an album of the ceremony and concert. Lucky Millinder was best man.

As a woman playing mostly raucous electric guitar for visual as well as aural impact in a primarily gospel setting, Wald called Tharpe "an unclassifiable figure." Tharpe enjoyed a drink and a flirt, and even played in nightclubs. Gospel scholar Horace Boyer said Tharpe "insisted upon a sound and a lifestyle of ambiguity."

Along the way, she influenced such artists as Isaac Hayes, Elvis Presley, Etta James, Jerry Lee Lewis, Bob Dylan, Odetta, and fellow Arkansawyers Johnny Cash and Sleepy LaBeef, while her blazing guitar stylings and flamboyant stage moves were echoed by guitar heroes Jimmy Page, Eric Clapton, Jimi Hendrix, Jeff Beck, and Pete Townshend.

Tharpe suffered a stroke in 1970, and had a leg amputated due to diabetes. She continued to perform until her death on October 9, 1973, at age 58, of further complications from diabetes. She is buried in Philadelphia, Pennsylvania, where she had settled. Tharpe didn't receive a proper headstone there until 2009, following fundraisers by her fans. She was featured on a U.S. postage stamp in 1998 and was inducted into the Rock & Roll Hall of Fame in 2018.

"Where are the female guitarists that have carried on her legacy? She was a hot dog player, she liked to do show-off moves . . . I don't know that the legacy exists," Wald concluded.

"She may be just a one-of-a-kind performer."

• **LISTENING** •

"Two Little Fishes And Five Loaves Of Bread" - Sister Rosetta Tharpe
"Didn't It Rain?" - Sister Rosetta Tharpe and Marie Knight with Sam Price Trio
"This Train" - Sister Rosetta Tharpe with Louis Jordan and His Tympany Five
"I Want A Tall Skinny Papa" - Lucky Millinder and His Orchestra with Rosetta Tharpe
"Strange Things Happening Every Day" - Sister Rosetta Tharpe
"Can't Sit Down" - Sister Rosetta Tharpe

VENA TOWNSEND
Rose Bud

songwriter, musician

Louvena Townsend was born in 1938 in Rose Bud and became a Northeast Arkansas honky tonk hero, although only issuing one single.

Part of a musical family, her parents were local musicians. Her father, Earl Lee, played fiddle, while her mother, Nancy Jane, was a singer like Louvena. She started young, making her radio debut at the age of nine. As a teenager in the 1950s, Townsend performed in the area with her brothers as the Townsend Family Band daily on Newport's KNBY station, known as the "Voice of the White River Valley."

By the late 1950s, Townsend had met Trumann native Arlen Vaden. With his wife Jackie, Vaden co-owned Vaden Records and ran a record store in Trumann. The Vadens, who married in 1951, also performed gospel music in the area as The Southern Gospel Singers and recorded their gospel programs for radio station broadcasts. Vaden Records started as a gospel music label doing steady mail-order sales, but the Vadens soon branched out their regional record label's sound to rockabilly, country, and beyond.

Arlen Vaden booked Townsend for her only known recording session for Vaden Records—or anyone else, for that matter—in 1959, at radio station KLCN on Second Street in Blytheville. The session featured Arlen Vaden and Fred Douglas on guitar, Roy Mullinax on bass, Billy Springer on steel guitar, and fellow Vaden Records artist Teddy Redell on piano.

The resulting single, with both sides written by Townsend, was released on Vaden later in 1959 as by Vena Townsend. On "I Walk (The Soles Off My Shoes)" her swooping, lonesome voice locks in with the honky tonk sound, her vocal cries mirroring the pain of lost love and echoing Hank Williams. Her song, "Too-Lonesome," is similarly aching.

Townsend's lone Vaden single sold locally but didn't break regionally. Arlen Vaden didn't pursue additional recording sessions for Townsend on the Vaden label. Townsend subsequently drifted away from the music business, got married, and for years was a factory worker. Arlen and Jackie Vaden divorced in the early 1960s, and Vaden Records folded. In the late 1980s,

Townsend rejoined her brothers Gerald and Dual in a Townsend family bluegrass trio.

Townsend's single is a solid selection from the tail end of the era of regional record labels recording local artists. The White County native's release remains an intriguing footnote in the history of Arkansas honky tonk music, as well as that of Trumann's Vaden label, and a glimpse into what could have been.

• LISTENING •
"Too-Lonesome" - Vena Townsend
"I Walk (The Soles Off My Shoes)" - Vena Townsend

SIPPIE WALLACE
Jefferson County

songwriter, pianist, singer

Sippie Wallace was one of the most celebrated musical performers of the 1920s in the United States.

Whether writing alone or with her brothers, she was known for her self-assured, often bawdy, lyrics and inventive blues songs. Born in the late 19th century, Wallace's songs had already been celebrated for generations of blues and early jazz fans by the time of her late 20th century comeback.

One of 13 children, she was born Beulah Thomas in Plum Bayou Township, north of Pine Bluff, in Jefferson County on November 1, 1898. The Thomases were very much a musical family. Her father was also a preacher, and she sang and played piano in his church. She later said she got the nickname "Sippie" in grade school because her teeth were so far apart she had to sip her drinks.

She grew up in Houston, Texas, which is why as a performer she was later promoted as "The Texas Nightingale." In the teens of the 20th century, she moved to New Orleans, Louisiana, living there with her musician brothers, George Jr. and young Hersal, until she married Matt Wallace in 1917. Through her brother George Jr.—a notable musician in his own right who was also a Plum Bayou native, born in 1883—she got hooked up with the emerging New Orleans jazz scene. Although less celebrated than their sister, both George Jr., and Hersal Thomas also became known as innovative writers and influential pianists in the development of jazz and blues.

In the 1920s, they all moved to Chicago, Illinois, which was becoming a commercial recording center for jazz and especially blues, rivaling New Orleans as a U.S. musical hub for those genres. Popular recorded blues in the 1920s was dominated by female vocalists, often with jazzy full band arrangements. For most people of the era, their introduction to blues music was through radio airplay, records, sheet music, and concert appearances by the genre's biggest stars: Bessie Smith, Ida Cox, Ma Rainey—and Sippie Wallace.

Through the decade, Wallace recorded more than 40 songs for Okeh Records, one of the premiere blues labels of its time. Her band on some of these now-classic blues sides included her New Orleans colleagues such as Louis Armstrong, King Oliver, Clarence Williams, and Sidney Bechet. All would become giants in the field of jazz, which had been branching off as its own genre distinct from blues.

Wallace wrote many of her songs herself, or with her brothers. George Jr. even handled the music publishing for the family with his Chicago-based George W. Thomas Music Co. In addition to his business savvy in handling music publishing, George Jr. is considered by many to be the father of boogie-woogie piano with his early genre-defining songs "The Fives" and "The Rocks."

Meanwhile, Wallace was honing a distinct songwriting voice all her own, becoming known for her sharp, self-possessed, often ribald, lyrics. And more than a century beyond, Wallace's songs remain highly regarded in the blues canon.

After a seemingly charmed career of being at the right place at the right time, Wallace faced tragedy in 1936, with the death of her husband, Matt, who was killed in a streetcar accident. Her brother, frequent collaborator, and music publisher, George Jr., died soon after. She said in later interviews that their deaths influenced her departure from performing blues. Further, their brother Hersal—also considered a forefather of blues and boogie piano in performance and style despite his young age—had died at age 19 of food poisoning some years before. The economic downturn of the Great Depression additionally hurt concert attendance and record and sheet music sales through the early 1930s. The commercial dominance of women in blues has never again matched the 1920s wave that Wallace rode.

Subsequently, Wallace retreated from music—but only secular music. She returned to her musical roots as a church organ player in Detroit, Michigan, where she'd be based for the rest of her life. "The Texas Nightingale"—the star of the Roaring Twenties who bragged onstage and on record that she was a "Mighty Tight Woman"—could now be found on Sundays playing at Detroit's Leland Baptist Church.

The mid-20th century resurgence of American folk and blues music worldwide saw many of Wallace's peers staging musical comebacks. By the late 1960s, Wallace was finally convinced by her old jazz and blues musician friends to do the same. She made concert appearances at such major events as the Newport Blues Festival, the Chicago Blues Festival, and the Ann Arbor Blues Festival. An album pairing Wallace with Victoria Spivey—who'd also been a part of the 1920s phenomenon of successful blueswomen, and who originally recorded with many of the same musicians as Wallace—was released in 1970. A stroke slowed Wallace's newfound momentum, but only temporarily.

Meanwhile, blues guitarist Bonnie Raitt—the Burbank, California-born daughter of Broadway actor-singer John Raitt—had been influenced by, and was a champion of, Wallace's music from early on in her musical career. Raitt had even included her own versions of two Wallace songs on her 1971 debut album and another on her 1972 follow-up.

But Raitt later said she didn't even know Wallace was still alive until, while on tour in London, she happened upon Wallace's album with Spivey. Raitt and Wallace finally met in 1972, and as Raitt became better known nationally, she continued introducing Wallace to an ever wider audience, with the pair often performing onstage together through the 1970s.

Raitt helped Wallace get a deal on Atlantic Records, and she produced Wallace's 1982 album, *Sippie*. By then,

Wallace and Raitt had been collaborators and friends for a decade. The two even appeared on television's *Late Night With David Letterman* to promote each other's new albums.

Explaining her many years away from recording, Wallace told show host David Letterman, "I didn't retire, I just took sick." She also claimed during the interview that George Jr. hid her from her old record company, Okeh, "because he thought I wouldn't use his songs." Wallace said, "My brother, George Thomas, he never did tell me, so I just thought they didn't want me."

For his part, Letterman notes that Wallace, then 83, "is the first guest we've ever had drinking a beer."

The album *Sippie* became a Grammy nominee and won a Handy award. It was also The Texas Nightingale's swan song. After nearly a century in music, the Arkansawyer and blues pioneer died in Detroit in 1986, on her November 1 birthday.

Having already stood the test of time, Sippie Wallace songs continue to be discovered by new generations of blues fans.

> • LISTENING •
>
> "Shorty George Blues" - Sippie Wallace
> "Special Delivery Blues" - Sippie Wallace
> "You Got To Know How" - Sippie Wallace
> "Mighty Tight Woman" - Sippie Wallace
> "A Man For Every Day In The Week" - Sippie Wallace
> "Mighty Tight Woman" - Bonnie Raitt
> "Women Be Wise" - Sippie Wallace and Bonnie Raitt

AFTERWORD

To see oneself in another is to see possibility, and in possibility, dreams begin.

The artists living in the pages of *From Almeda to Zilphia: Arkansas Women Who Transformed American Popular Song*—mighty women breaking new ground and creating lasting contributions from country to classical to the foundations of rock 'n' roll—open the door to an endless world of possibilities. This book will no doubt speak to some little girl, somewhere in Arkansas, no matter her background or what she looks like, and tell her, *There is a place for you. A big, beautiful, important place for you.*

When I moved to Nashville, Tennessee, more than 20 years ago, I heard a lot of things, like "Don't sing your own demos. Men can't hear through a woman singing." (Demos being the recorded version of a song used to play for artists or their team.) I heard "Your songs are too sad. They'll never be picked up." "Okay, but you're not an artist. You'll never play The Opry."

The first two songs I had recorded were ballads sung by Alan Jackson and Randy Travis from my demos. To date, I've put out more than four albums of music as an artist and had the honor of playing The Opry over 20 times. I've seen my dreams and more come true. I say these things not to toot my own proverbial horn, but to say that oftentimes you will encounter those who will try and tell you why things are not possible, why you cannot accomplish whatever dream has been set in your heart.

I have found the best remedy for this is to read the stories of brilliant rebels who have come before. Find yourself among those who have challenged what is possible, have grabbed a hold of "yes" in a world that can appear to be full of "no." And while all outstanding artists may be cut from that cloth, having a collection of varied women's stories adds rich dimension to the archetypal story of success and music stardom. Sharing such powerful stories will no doubt allow more of us to see ourselves reflected and therefore more easily see the path forward.

As a young girl, I remember finding K.T. Oslin's music and being enthralled. I had heard she was born in Arkansas, and from where I sat on my grandparents' blue shag den carpet, watching her on their rabbit ear-antennaed television set, I felt a connection. I would rent her collection of music videos and study them intently. In junior high, I was assigned a project on Maya Angelou. Immediately, I was taken with her voice, with her songs and poetry, with how deftly she could carve a picture with her words. I traveled to Stamps where she spent time as a child, just so I could breathe the same air and walk the same roads. I felt a geographical and musical kinship to these artists and others mentioned in this book, and I have no doubt that their successes emboldened me, made me feel from the start that the stars were within reach.

When I wanted to put my thoughts on a blank page, to

AFTERWORD

stand in front of my peers and present my work, to move to Nashville, or to do whatever might come next, it did not seem so impossible because I had seen a groove cut to follow. I'm so proud to be a small part of Arkansas's magnificent musical legacy, to continue the work of these amazing artists, and to add my voice to the song.

Not too long ago, I was a little girl in Conway, poring over albums, biographies, and music videos with a music-shaped dream growing in my heart.

Today, I am a woman carrying the flag for my home state's creative abilities far and wide. I still face challenges and those trying to place limitations on me, but as the saying goes, "the horrors persist, but so do I." When I feel myself beating my head against the wall of resistance and exclusion, I draw comfort, strength, and inspiration from the artists who have persevered and thrived before me.

Here's to the next generation of Arkansawyers and the beautiful music they will make.

—**Erin Enderlin**

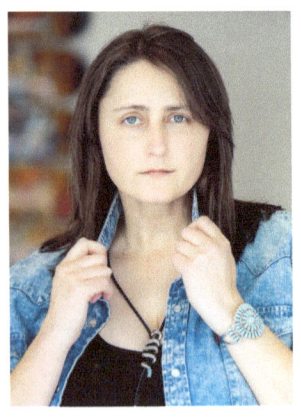

Erin Enderlin is at the forefront of current artists rooted in country music's rich history. A frequent performer on The Grand Ole Opry, her acclaimed 2017 album *Whiskeytown Crier* cemented her as a literary songwriter and superb vocal stylist with a knack for sharply drawn, often sad, characters. Her follow-up album *Faulkner County* made *Rolling Stone* magazine's top 20 Country / Americana Albums of the Year in 2019, and she was featured as a breakthrough artist in the 2020 *American Currents* exhibit at the Country Music Hall of Fame and Museum. As writer of Alan Jackson's "Monday Morning Church," Lee Ann Womack's "Last Call," Luke Bryan's "You Don't Know Jack," and a host of other songs by Randy Travis, Reba McEntire, Terri Clark, Gene Watson, Willie Nelson, Trisha Yearwood, and others, she's a go-to writer for stars looking for heavyweight country with classic panache.

Author **Stephen Koch** is an award-winning journalist in both broadcasting and print, with a focus on the culture and history of Arkansas and surrounding states. A songwriter, musician, author, playwright, and cartoonist, Koch is also host and writer of *Arkansongs*, a weekly feature syndicated on public radio stations throughout the Midsouth.

Illustrator **Katherine Strause** is a working artist and educator. She exhibits nationally and her work is in many public and private collections. Strause is the retired Chair of the Art Department and Professor of Painting at Henderson State University. She holds a Bachelor of Art from the University of Arkansas at Little Rock and a Master of Fine Arts from Southern Illinois University at Edwardsville.

Arkansongs is an award-winning music heritage program syndicated for more than a quarter-century to hundreds of thousands of listeners on public radio stations throughout the U.S. Midsouth. Written and hosted by musician and author Stephen Koch and produced by Keith Merckx, *Arkansongs* examines the people, places, and events that have made this region key in forming the musical vernacular that has influenced the world.

Et Alia Press is a "small press for big voices" publishing award-winning nonfiction and children's books in Little Rock since 2010. It is owned and run by Erin Wood, editor of and a contributor to *Scars: An Anthology* and author of *Women Make Arkansas: Conversations with 50 Creatives*. Find her at erinwood.com and the Press at etaliapress.com.